Get to Know
Cat Breeds

Ga.

Over 40 Best-Known Breeds

Contents

Pedigree Cats › 4

Cat Breeds › 10

All breeds officially recognized by the Fédération International Féline (FIFe) are profiled in this section. Breeds have been sorted into groups according to coat length and origin.

Persian and Exotic Shorthair

› 10

Semilonghair Breeds

› 16

Short-Haired Breeds and Somali

> **36**

Oriental Breeds

> **76**

Breeds Recognized by the World Cat Federation

Not Recognized by FIFe

> **86**

Living With a Pedigreed Cat > 106

Finding a Reputable Breeder **106**

The Purchase Agreement **107**

Basic Needs **108**

Vaccinations and Deworming **109**

Grooming and Hygiene **110**

Claw Care **114**

Traveling With Your Cat **116**

Cat Associations **117**

Questionnaire > 120

Glossary > 122

Further Reading > 124
(Books and Internet Addresses)

Index > 126

Copyright > 128

Pedigree Cats

Tabby, domestic tiger, tomcat, furball, mouser, pussycat, kitty . . . cats are known by many names, each one trying to describe their many fascinating qualities. Although domestic cats do not vary in size like the canine breeds do—for example, the four-pound Chihuahua versus the one-hundred-fifty-pound Great Dane—the many cat breeds are just as rich in variety.

At first glance, the Norwegian forest cat and the Oriental shorthair might look very different, but they have more in common than one might think. Although a Persian cat has a sturdier build and a much broader face than a Siamese cat, and the fur types are different, their overall appearance still resembles that of their wildcat ancestors. There is a reason for this: making specific changes to the wildcat's typical appearance was never really the aim of cat breeders. This is totally different from breeding dogs, whereby each dog is bred for his physical characteristics in order to perform a specific task, for example, a hunting dog.

Although the body shape of every cat breed is relatively similar, there are some slight differences in build, which are due mainly to the climate, among other factors. Cats from colder regions will usually have sturdier builds and fairly long fur. Cats in warmer regions tend to be leaner with mostly short fur and usually do not have undercoats.

In the second half of the nineteenth century, cat shows were popular, but you could admire just three cat breeds: European short-haired cats with strong, sturdy builds; long-haired cats from Southwest Asia; and the graceful, slender beauties from the Far East. Today, there are about one hundred different cat breeds recognized by various cat associations, which differ greatly from one another. In this book, you will find a detailed description of each breed recognized by the international umbrella organization Fédération International Féline (FIFe), plus many more. There are three main builds: slender, medium, and large.

› Slender Build

These breeds are seen as classy and elegant. Modern Siamese cats are one example of this build. In recent decades, cat lovers have placed increasing value on the extremely slender, elongated physique. However, modern breeding has divided fans of this body type into two camps: those who are fans of the modern type's wedge-shaped head, very large ears, and extremely slender physique, and those who prefer the original bigger-boned, fuller-faced Siamese cat.

› Medium and Large Build

Among the officially recognized breeds, there are many cat breeds that fall into the medium build category, such as the Thai cat, Birman, and Turkish Angora. In the United States and Europe, large-framed breeds have become increasingly popular: the sturdy Maine coon, which can weigh up to thirty-five pounds, and the stately looking Norwegian forest cat are among the most popular purebred cats.

› Something for Everyone

Whether you favor a slim, medium, or large breed is a matter of personal taste. All three varieties of cat breeds have their individual charm and appeal.

When choosing a cat, it is a good idea to go not just on appearance, but to also pay attention to the individual character of the cat because it is important that your cat's personality is right for you. Do you prefer a feisty cat or one that is calmer?

Sociable Cats

New is interesting: sociable cats are not afraid of new people. They will quickly get over their initial uncertainty and behave in an open, friendly manner, encouraging people to pet them. This type of cat is interested in everything, loves to play, and can become quite pushy if he feels neglected. However, you, as a human, are not allowed to exercise the same right. The cat will always determine when he wants a cuddle from you, not the other way around! Pushy people are not popular with this type of cat.

Shy Cats

Although most Somalis can be described as playful and lively, they are particularly cautious around new people. Somalis tend to choose one or two people to be the center of their world. Nevertheless, they do get along well in a group but always express their individuality.

Korats and Ceylons have a reputation of being quiet, affectionate creatures. But they are suspicious about loud, intrusive people. These felines prefer sensitive, calm cat owners.

Shyness can also occur in cats that have had bad experiences. Stray cats, cats from animal shelters, or cats that have had several owners may avoid human contact, often due to a fear of loss in the case of a neglected cat, for example. A person who takes on a cat like this needs to give his or her cat a lot of time, patience, and understanding.

Quiet Cats

Ragdolls and exotic shorthairs have a reputation for being gentle and affectionate. Although they like to play and take an active interest in their surroundings, they belong to the quieter members of the feline family. Ragdolls and exotic shorthairs usually tolerate children and other pets very well.

Hectic, noisy households are generally not ideal for the Russian blue. Although some very different traits have been known in this breed (from lively to extremely quiet), the majority tend to be reserved and sensitive.

Scottish folds and Manx cats are also known for their calm temperaments. The Scottish fold is quite happy to live his life indoors and is very tolerant of people. His strangely formed ears can often cause misunderstandings with other cats—the ears lie permanently flat against the head, which can be interpreted as a sign of aggression. The "tailless" Manx cats and the Japanese bobtails are much loved breeds because they make very peaceful members of a household.

Cats with more temperamental characters are sensitive and delicate; they do not belong in noisy households. A stressful atmosphere can cause serious behavioral problems for these fickle cats. They are best suited to experienced owners who are more sensitive to the needs of their temperamental pets.

Pedigreed or Mixed-Breed Cat?

Bringing home a cat means making a very important decision: should you choose a pedigreed cat from a breeder or a mixed-breed cat from a shelter? Well, you may think it does not matter—a cat is a cat, right? What is the difference? Actually, there are several major differences between these two options.

› Each As Lovable As the Next

But before the differences between breeds and individual cats are discussed, the author would like to emphasize that each domestic cat is valuable and deserves respect and unconditional affection from his owner. No cat is more important than another simply because he cost one thousand dollars, for example. A stray cat from a shelter can give his new family just as much joy as a regal kitten from a prestigious pedigreed background.

› Adventures in the Wild

But of course, there are some significant differences in characteristics between breeds, and although these do not apply to every single cat, they are generally accepted observations.

Many cats, even if they do not belong to a particular breed, appreciate their independence and have a strong desire for freedom. They want to leave the house or apartment at will in order to experience adventures in "the wild." However, the outside world is a dangerous place for a cat. He can contract illnesses, be hit by a car, be attacked by other animals, or be harmed by cruel people. Make sure your cat has plenty of toys and things to do indoors so he does not get bored and act out.

Daytime adventures in the yard (under supervision) and spending the evening snuggled up in a blanket are popular activities for every cat.

› Happy Indoor Cats

Owners who do not want their cats to roam outdoors can choose a purebred cat or a mixed-breed cat. Some cats do not have a great desire for freedom because they have only ever lived indoors.

› Combing Your Cat

A big difference between mixed-breed and purebred cats is grooming requirements. Grooming is not usually necessary for short-haired breeds, which usually have neat, easy-to-care-for coats. Semilonghair or long-haired breeds usually require intensive grooming. Persians need to be combed or brushed daily, and semilonghair cats should be groomed at least once or twice a week to keep their fur in good condition.

› Pedigree (The Family Tree)

When we talk about pedigreed cats, we are talking about purebred cats whose lineages have been documented. A cat may very well be a purebred, but without the documentation to back it up, you cannot be sure. When buying a pedigreed kitten, reputable cat breeders must provide you with the official papers, which is also considered your proof of ownership. The document should contain the name and address of the association at which the kitten is registered, registration number, name and address of the breeder, name of the kitten, its sex, date of birth, color, and the exact breed. Furthermore, depending on the rules of the association your kitten is registered with, the pedigree may list the parents, grandparents, great-grandparents, and great-great-grandparents, including the names, colors, and registration numbers of these animals. If there are relatives of the pedigreed kitten that are not registered, this should be clearly indicated.

Besides the Fédération International Féline (FIFe), there are several other international, national, and regional cat registries, including the Cat Fanciers' Association (CFA), The International Cat Association (TICA), the American Cat Fanciers Association (ACFA), the Cat Fanciers' Federation (CFF), and the World Cat Federation (WCF). Each organization has its own breed standards and may or may not recognize a certain breed.

Titles and Awards

The pedigree also includes a section in which the new cat owner can enter any awards won at shows. Show titles should be registered with an official association. For example, some of the titles awarded by FIFe include Champion (CH; unaltered cats) or Premier (PR; altered cats), International Champion/Premier (IC/IP), Grand International Champion/Premier (GIC/GIP), and Supreme Champion/Premier (SC/SP). The Cat Fanciers' Association titles include Regional Winner (RG), National Winner (NW), Grand Champion/Premier (GC/GP), and International Division Winner (DW). The acquired titles should be properly registered and recorded for the next generation of young pedigrees. Any breeding changes to the pedigree must not be made without authorization. Color changes to the breed, for example, can only be approved by a judge and a committee appointed by the relevant breeding association. Otherwise, the pedigree will be invalid.

Pedigrees are regulated by the appropriate cat association. Breeders must follow the breeding rules of their specific organization. If you buy a pedigreed kitten, you should ensure it comes from a reputable and regulated breeder.

Breeding Regulations

There are many breeding rules for each association. For example, cats should not breed until they are one year old, and a female is not allowed to breed until at least three months after her last litter. The number of litters is limited to a maximum of two within twelve months.

The mating of siblings is only allowed after a thorough process of authorization. This process requires the breeder to demonstrate how the mating will lead to an improvement of the breed. The resulting offspring only receive their pedigrees after a full medical report of each kitten has been submitted. The same procedure applies when cats with only nine or fewer different ancestors in their genealogies are mated. Crosses between different breeds are generally prohibited. They are only acceptable if they will have a positive influence on the breed.

The regulations of these cat associations are not just to regulate the appearance of the breed, but also the welfare of the breed. Unregulated breed crosses, inbreeding, breeding cats with genetic defects, and exploitatively bred animals are to be avoided. Keep in mind that breeders who do not belong to a reputable association are not subject to official breeding regulations.

Male or Female?

However, a pedigreed cat with a family tree does not tell the whole story. You should also consider the sex of the cat before making the final decision. Should you choose a male or female cat? Apart from the obvious physical difference in size with males being larger than females, how else do they differ from one another? This question should be considered by a responsible prospective cat owner prior to adoption.

Breeding Your Cat

Female cats are the better choice if your aim is to breed kittens in your own home. Those who want to breed their cats are better off with a female cat than a caterwauling, scent-marking male that will try to escape to pester all the prospective females in the neighborhood!

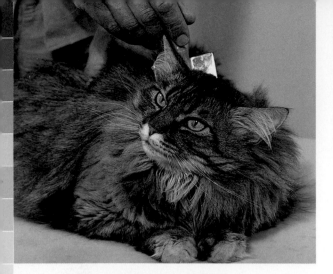

◄ Some breeds require regular grooming.

▼ Male or female cat? The most important thing is to choose the cat that is best for you.

Wallpaper, furniture, carpets, and curtains will be sprayed with urine, and even though not all potent males scent-mark, this foul odor is a constant threat.

Spaying or neutering your cat will go a long way to help permanently eliminate this bad habit. Obviously, your cat-breeding dreams will not be fulfilled if you decide to neuter your cat. After being altered, most animals will stop scent-marking. However, strong sexual stimuli, for example, the sight of a prospective female cat, can still provoke scent-marking from a neutered male. Also, the sudden threat of an unknown cat in the neighborhood may lead to similar behavior.

Apart from neutering, there are some other approaches, such as training and medication, that might put a stop to scent-marking. But these methods do not guarantee success.

Consistent training measures do provide relief from this problem in some cases. However, you need to catch the culprit red-handed and immediately reprimand him in a firm voice. Moderate use of a water gun or a loud clap of your hands can sometimes be effective as well.

❯ Scent-Marking Males

So what about the males? Perhaps you wish to breed cats and want to acquire a stud for this purpose. Your home will become a breeding ground and provide a base for matings. If he breeds successfully, he will enjoy an excellent reputation and may be sought after by other breeders with female cats. Regular health checks, which prospective females are also required to have, are all part of the routine for any serious stud owners.

However, studs do not come without their problems. A scent-marking stud can make a strong stench in your house. Not only will this be an assault to your nose, but it will also probably keep all your friends away!

The places that have been scent-marked must always be cleaned immediately and thoroughly so that the odor is not left behind. This is not an easy task because the odor is very persistent, and cats have a very good sense of smell.

Some scent-marks can be eliminated using aromatherapy oils diluted with water, such as citronella, orange, or lemon. Commercial odor removers prove unsuccessful in many cases.

There is also a medical solution when all else fails. Treatment using progestogens (orally or by injection) has proved to be successful in some males; however, these may only last three to four months and must be re-administered on a regular basis, so they are not a permanent solution. There are also serious side effects. Certain pheromones, biological chemicals that influence behavior, can also help eliminate the problem. Veterinarians and pet therapists will be able to advise you what is best.

› Scent-Marking Females

Unfortunately, owners of female cats must also deal with scent-marking behavior. Some females scent-mark more than males! If your female cat is a notorious scent-marker, you can try using the previously described methods to solve the problem.

Females that have not been spayed put on a very special display when in heat, which can drive family members and the cat herself crazy. She tilts her head at an angle, rubs her body on the ground, rolls around in a dramatic fashion, and sticks her rear end up in the air. She also meows loudly to attract a willing mate.

On average, cats reach sexual maturity between the ages of four and seven months. For large breeds, such as the Maine coon, sexual maturity comes much later.

› Spaying and Neutering

If you are simply looking for a loving addition to your family, a cat that rubs his or her head against you in a friendly, affectionate manner and does not display any of the characteristics of a cat in heat, you should get your pet neutered or spayed as soon as his or her physical development permits. Once altered, both males and females become calmer, cuddlier, and more sociable. In the beginning, you should simply pick the kitten you feel is both drawn to you and suitable for you no matter the sex.

› So Many Beautiful Breeds

But enough of the preface. It is time to open the curtains on the variety of gorgeous breeds in the feline world. On the following pages, more than fifty breeds are waiting to be discovered.

In the first four parts of the book are concise descriptions of the breeds officially recognized by the Fédération International Féline (FIFe). The fifth part is reserved for popular breeds whose standards have been created by the World Cat Federation (WCF), among others. In the United States, Australia, and other parts of the world, some cat breeds are recognized by individual organizations, but not by the large umbrella organizations. Some of these breeds are, at present, extremely rare.

A short description of the standard is given for each cat breed, which is an excerpt from the original standards outlined by the various cat associations. The complete official standards can be obtained from the FIFe or the WCF, or on their official Web sites. You may also want to check out the most well-known cat organization in the United States, the Cat Fanciers' Association (CFA).

Persian and Exotic Shorthair

◄ The Persian chinchilla is, for many, the crowning achievement of this breed.

► Because the very long fur of a Persian becomes easily matted, this breed is only suited to life indoors.

Persian cats are still high on the popularity scale of pedigreed cats. This is a well-deserved status: the Persian is one of the best-known breeds in the world. Persians are not only popular due to their appearance, but they have also had a genetic influence on a variety of other attractive breeds. Without Persians, which were mostly bred in England, there would not be so many other impressive varieties of beautiful cat breeds around today.

The beginnings of this enchanting breed can be traced back to the 1870s. In those days, soft doll-faced Persians were very rare and mainly belonged to members of the aristocracy. Queen Victoria was known to be a proud owner of a pair of blue Persian cats.

❯ Persian in a Summer Coat

The American exotic shorthair breed originates from the British Persian breed. The standards for the exotics resemble that of the Persians almost exactly, except

exotics are short-haired cats. For owners who do not have time to groom their cats every day, the exotic shorthair is an ideal alternative.

It was not only the Persian that contributed to the origin of the exotic shorthair in the 1950s and 1960s. The pioneers of the American exotic shorthairs initially used the Russian blue and Birman breeds to create new breeds. This was not the original intention, however. Persian cats were bred with American short-haired breeds in order to improve their fur quality. In addition, breeders experimented with the gene of the long-haired silver Persian. The crossing experiments of the Persians with short-haired breeds led to the beginning of the exotic shorthair.

❯ A Cat of Many Colors

What is astonishing about category I of the FIFe breeds is the almost overwhelming variety of colors recognized for the Persian and exotic shorthairs: white, black, blue, red, cream, chocolate, lilac; all variations of tortoiseshell, bicolor, harlequin, or van; tabby; and silver or golden. The variations of silver are chinchilla (the lighter variant) and shaded silver (the darker variant). Added to this impressive list are the beautiful colorpoints. Fans of this breed may find it very hard to pick their favorite color, and who could blame them?

Except for the coat length, exotics and Persians are alike not only in terms of physique, but there are also clear parallels between characteristics of these cats. Neither belongs to the hyperactive, talkative, and lively cat breeds. These cats like to take life at a slower pace, which also means they are not terribly playful. Anybody familiar with the ancient nobility of these cats will know they make a quiet, calm family member that loves to sit for hours with her people on the couch. A hectic household does not mesh well with the leisurely lifestyle of these breeds.

The same goes for all-weather activities. Fans of the outdoors and Persian cats are the worst possible combination. Anyone who believes cats should be out playing in the yard would be better off owning one of the short-haired breeds. The lush fur of the Persian tends to mat. Outdoor adventures would turn this cat's fur into

a disaster area. Small twigs, burrs, garden dirt, and other souvenirs can only be removed with great difficulty. There are some exotic shorthairs that are slightly more suited to the occasional outdoor adventure, but these are still not really your typical outdoor cats.

> Avoid Extremes

The Persians and exotic shorthairs have long been a popular subject of discussion. The topic of debate is the extreme breeding practices that are clearly detrimental to the cats' health. Over time, the noses became flatter and migrated higher and higher on the face. In the United States, so-called "peke-faced" Persians came into vogue, with the nose placed between the eyes. The consequences of these extreme forms of breeding can be fatal. The animal has difficulty breathing, constantly encrusted eyes, and a runny nose, which has caused what can only be described as terrible disabilities in some Persians.

Fortunately, the trend is now moving backward again. Moderate breeds with less problems are more in demand than ill-bred creatures with impaired quality of life—and that can only be a good thing. The queen of pedigreed cats should remain what she once was: an enchantingly beautiful, affectionate, healthy cat.

Exotic Shorthair >14
Persian >12

< Exotic shorthairs are easier to care for than Persians.

11

Persian

Build: medium to large, stocky

Head: broad, round; wide-set, small ears decorated with tufts of fur; broader around the muzzle; short, broad nose

Eyes: large, round, expressive; color according to coat color

Body: stocky, muscular; short legs, broad chest

Tail: short, bushy

Coat: long and thick with a silky, fine texture

Color: white, black, blue, red, cream, chocolate, lilac, all tortoiseshell variations, all bicolor variations, harlequin, van, tabby, silver, golden, colorpoint

A royal beauty—the classic long-haired cat breed

For some, Persian cats are the epitome of the pedigreed cat, but for others, in terms of expense and maintenance, they are considered a bit of a nightmare! Opinion is divided on the Persian, yet they have still managed to remain extremely popular and are seen as a status symbol for many. For those who desire to own a pet with luxurious fur, a beautiful doll-like face, and an easygoing temperament, the Persian is the perfect choice.

Many other cat breeds owe their looks and heritage to the Persian. This breed of purring beauties began in England. It is presumed that the first long-haired Persian came from Turkey to England. These unusual exports were known as Angora cats and were actually more similar to today's Turkish Angora. Around the same time, another breed

came from Persia to England and these cats had very rounded heads and denser fur. The two breeds were mated because they were both long-haired breeds and so were very well matched. At the time, long-haired cats were a rarity and attracted the interest of the British royal family. Queen Victoria soon had a pair of these long-haired beauties to call her own, and many cat lovers were eager to own a Persian. However, at the time, they were still rare and difficult to obtain.

Around 1870, the breeding of these Persians became more intensive as breeders aimed to improve the cute, doll-like appearance of these cats. Since then, one of the most influential cat breeds of all time was created—the Persian as we know it today. They are now bred in many different colors.

Cat of Your Dreams

For many cat lovers, the Persian is the
ultimate dream. At cat shows, curious
onlookers crowd around the cages
containing these magnificent beauties,
and there is scarcely another breed that
draws so many admiring comments.
The Persian is truly one of the most
striking representatives of the feline
world. The remarkably prolific breeding
of these cats does carry risks, however:
not every breeder is reputable, and not
every breeder cares for the health of his
or her kittens. Therefore, you should
spend a lot of time carefully selecting
the right breeder and examine the
kittens thoroughly when you visit them.
There is another factor you should also
consider before making the decision to
purchase a Persian—grooming.

Grooming

The meticulous care of the Persian
fur is an important issue. Anyone
who dreams of owning one of these
long-haired beauties must be prepared
to schedule daily grooming into her
everyday life. Otherwise, the cat will
suffer with tangled fur, skin problems,
and eventually will have to have her
fur shaved off completely. For proud
Persian owners, shaving off the fur
is simply unthinkable, and it could
take months for the beautiful, dense
fur coat to return. Persians shed their
fur twice a year and during this time,
you will need to increase the amount
of grooming. Silver-colored varieties
become temporarily darker than usual
during the shedding phase.

Cats are neat and tidy
animals. They dedicate
themselves to daily grooming
and spend hours keeping their
fur clean. Most short-haired
cats do not need any help with
grooming; however, long-haired
cats need human assistance to
keep their fur in good condition.
Persians are a prime example of
this. If this long-haired breed
is not groomed daily, this will
cause the cat hygiene problems
due to the matted fur. Therefore,
grooming your Persian is an
essential part of her daily care.

Exotic Shorthair

Build: medium to large, squat

Head: round, solid, well-proportioned, broad skull; rounded forehead; full cheeks; short, broad nose; round, wide-set ears

Eyes: large, round, open, wide set, expressive, clear color

Body: stocky, short legs; broad chest; solid and well-muscled shoulders and back

Tail: short, dense fur; rounded tip

Coat: dense, plush, soft; stands up on end

Color: same colors as the Persian

An exotic is a Persian with short fur. She is easier to groom and care for.

Are you someone who has always dreamt of owning a Persian but the thought of the daily twenty-minute grooming session has put you off? If so, the exotic shorthair breed may be the one for you. Exotics do need to be brushed on a regular basis but the time required for grooming is far more tolerable than for a long-haired Persian. The short-haired versions of the Persian breed are similar to their long-haired relatives in appearance and character, but they come in a slightly different package. The thick, soft, plush coat is like a teddy bear's. It does not tend to knot, and it takes very little maintenance to keep your short-haired cat looking her best.

These short-haired Persians have not been around nearly as long as their long-haired counterparts. Exotic shorthairs were bred in the 1950s and 1960s. In the United States, home of the exotic shorthair, Persians were crossed with American shorthairs. The aim of this pairing was to create a breed that improved on the American shorthair, with a rounder head and silkier fur.

In 1966, the Cat Fanciers' Association (CFA) advised a crossing between Persians and American shorthairs. The breed standard was based on that of the Persian. At first, only the hybrids of the American shorthairs and Persians were allowed, but the CFA soon authorized other short-haired breeds to be bred with Persians to create the new exotic shorthair breed.

On the Rise

In the beginning, the plush "teddy bear" with the doll-like face offered a picture far from the ideal, but soon this breed won over cat fans. Unfortunately, this popularity did not change the fact that many American Persian breeders feared for the purebred image of the Persian.

In the past, breeding the Persian and the exotic shorthair together was a prerequisite for a large gene pool and a solid breeding base. It was thought that mating two exotic shorthairs would never create a satisfactory alternative; cats with a good coat quality were always a result of exotic shorthair and Persian matings.

Today, exotic shorthairs can still be paired with Persians to increase the gene pool and compensate for any physical defects. However, in contrast to before, exotic shorthairs are now often bred together. Because of the Persian blood in the exotic shorthair, two exotic shorthairs can cometimes produce a long-haired kitten.

Ideal House Cats

These short-haired kitties enjoy low-key activities such as purring on the living room couch, curling up on their owner's lap for a snooze, or testing their claws on the scratching post. This is not to suggest that they are lazy or lethargic. They are just quieter than other cats and have a more relaxed, easygoing approach to life.

The balanced, peaceful nature of this cozy, cuddly pet makes this breed the ideal indoor cat. Exotic shorthairs are sweet and affectionate and do not tend to give their owners any trouble. From time to time, they like to play and run around, but their bursts of energy are not on the same level of the Oriental breeds. The quiet little voice of the exotic shorthair enhances his sweet and friendly nature. Exotic shorthair fans love the character of this short-haired version of the Persian. This breed displays a calm, peaceful, sociable nature with plenty of curiosity, affection, and robustness, provided the cat is from a responsible breeder who has bred the cat in the best way possible—with plenty of love, affection, and health care.

A small area in your yard, an outdoor enclosure, or a safe and secure balcony are a good idea for this lovable cat, but this is not a must. Exotic shorthairs will quite happily adapt to life as indoor cats.

15

Semilonghair Breeds

‹ A Turkish Van is a rare and ancient breed.

› The Maine coon (bottom of next page) is the most popular of all the semilonghair felines.

Semilonghair cat breeds, or category II as it has been named by FIFe, consist of the following ten breeds: American curl longhair, American curl shorthair, Maine coon, Norwegian forest cat, ragdoll, Birman, Siberian forest cat, Turkish Angora, Turkish Van, and the Neva masquerade, which is the colorpoint variation of the Siberian forest cat breed.

The coat length of each semilonghair breed varies quite a bit, which is easy to see when comparing the American curl longhair and American curl shorthair, for example. Most coats lengths are somewhere in between these two extremes. In any case, their fur is not as long as that of a Persian nor as short as any of the short-haired breeds.

There must be something about these category II cats: in recent years, semilonghair cats have experienced a huge increase in popularity. In the United States, Maine coons and ragdolls are the most popular breeds in this category.

› The Stars of the Show

None of the other semilonghair breeds can possibly compete with the popularity of the Maine coons and ragdolls. These gentle giants have stolen hearts all over the country. The popularity of these breeds has met with disadvantages, however, as breeders were quick to get on the bandwagon and meet demand for these cats, without having the knowledge required to breed them properly and responsibly. Poor coat quality, behavioral problems, and health problems have plagued these two breeds as well as others.

American Curl >18

Birman >26

Maine Coon >20

Neva Masquerade >30

Norwegian Forest Cat >22

Ragdoll >24

Siberian Forest Cat >28

Turkish Angora >32

Turkish Van >34

Fortunately, there are also good breeders who value the health and strength of their kittens. When all breeds of cat are responsibly bred with the right knowledge, they can produce truly wonderful kittens that light up the feline stage. It really is worth seeking out such reputable breeders when choosing your pedigreed cat.

› Easy to Care For

One of the factors likely to please fans of these breeds is how easy it is to care for these cats. While it cannot be claimed that none of these breeds will ever have matted fur, it does not need constant brushing. Once or twice a week is enough. And if that seems like too much trouble then your best bet is a short-haired breed, which needs virtually no grooming whatsoever.

Owners of semilonghair cats should pay particular attention to the fur on the abdomen, inner thighs, armpits, and behind the ears. These areas tend to get tangled and become difficult to smooth out. The amount of grooming required depends on the individual fur length and texture, and also whether you want your cat to be exhibited as a show cat. If you want your cat to have show-standard fur, you will need to learn some special grooming techniques.

› A Fan of Nature

Although each individual cat is special with unique characteristics, it is generally the case that most semilonghair cats love nature and the outdoors. Siberians, Turkish Vans, Turkish Angoras,

Norwegian forest cats, and Maine coons all love to explore the great outdoors and will appreciate being allowed to roam around in outdoor enclosures or on secured balconies.

In terms of temperament, these furry friends are fairly lively. They are not quite as restless as the Oriental breeds, but they are certainly not dozy by any means. Owners should provide these cats with plenty of sturdy toys and a good, stable cat tree to play on.

With their sociable personalities, the semilonghair cat breeds make ideal family cats. Children, dogs, and other animals are usually well tolerated, and these breeds easily adapt to a lively household.

American Curl

Build: medium

Head: longer than it is broad, wedge shaped; slightly curved side profile

Eyes: walnut shaped; oval-shaped upper lids, rounded bottom lids

Body: elongated, slender; moderately developed muscles

Tail: long, broad at the base, slightly rounded tip, bushy

Coat: silky, usually of medium density; fur lies flat; minimal undercoat

Colors: all colors and patterns

This breed has curly ears, for those who love a cat breed with a twist.

The most striking feature about this breed is the ears that curl backward toward the head. Otherwise, the American curl is quite similar to the domestic cat from which it descended, although coat lengths do vary from cat to cat. His friendly, affectionate nature makes this cat a great housemate, and his remarkable intelligence presents many unexpected challenges for his owner.

The American curl breed was said to be a spontaneous mutation of a normal domestic cat. Presumably then, cats with curly ears have always existed, and no one attempted to breed them specifically until the early 1980s. A couple in Southern California came across a long-haired black cat with unusual ears at the entrance of a garage. They took the stray cat home with them and founded the American curl breed.

Recognition

The breed was so successful that shortly afterward, long-haired and short-haired curls were bred. The largest cat associations soon acknowledged the existence of these unusual looking cats. In 1987, The International Cat Association (TICA) officially recognized the breed, as did the Cat Fanciers' Association (CFA) four years later. The FIFe included this breed in their categories in 2002. Nowadays, this charming curly-eared cat exists in almost all colors and patterns, including black, blue, chocolate, cinnamon, lilac, and fawn in all combinations (bicolor, tricolor, tabby point). There is no relation between eye color and coat color except blue eyes are required in Siamese pointed cats. The popularity of this breed just grew and grew, which would not be a surprise to anyone who has come into contact with one of these enchanting cats. His gentle nature and friendly character will have you wrapped around his little paw. Intelligence and a strong willingness to learn guarantee a lot of fun, and thanks to the breed's adaptability, these cats tend to get along well with other pets.

Care

The coat of this medium-sized, slender breed is easy to care for but should be brushed regularly to keep its silky sheen. During the annual shedding season, long-haired American curls require more frequent brushing. According to the breed standard, the fur should lie flat and have a minimal undercoat, and the tail should be fluffy and feathered. The ruff, or collar, of the American curl is not as pronounced as that of the Norwegian forest cat and Maine coon.

The breed standard of an American curl is, of course, also very specific about the ears. The ears should not curl more than 180 degrees or less than 90 degrees. The lower part of the medium-height ears is made up of stiff cartilage, and this section should be wide and open. The tips of the ears, about one-third of the total ear length, should be curved but flexible enough to be straightened up. The ears should not meet in the middle. Another important factor is the symmetry of the ears. Imagine a line between the tips of the ears. The middle point of this imaginary line should fall exactly in the middle of the skull. Finally, the American curl should have tufts of fur growing from his ears to give the complete picture.

These cheerful curly-eared pets are ideal for people who are looking for a cat they can develop a special bond with. And you will need to be slightly thick-skinned as the owner of one of these cats because their distinguishing feature may attract some interesting comments!

Maine Coon

Build: large, strong

Head: medium size, square; concave profile; curved forehead; high cheekbones

Eyes: large, wide set, slightly oval; clear color

Body: elongated, rectangular; strong bones; well-developed muscles; broad chest

Tail: wide at base but pointed at tip with long, flowing fur

Coat: dense, medium-length outercoat; dense undercoat; shorter on the head, shoulders, legs; shaggy on the hind legs, neck, and belly

Colors: all except colorpoint, chocolate, lilac, cinnamon, and fawn

Superstrong—this kitty is extra large!

This feline Goliath is often called the "gentle giant" of the cat world, a name that refers not just to his impressive size but also to his lovely nature. His weight is often highly exaggerated, with some reporting highs of forty pounds or more, but despite the fairy tales, this really is one large kitty cat. When placed next to a Norwegian forest cat or Siberian cat, the Maine coon leaves the others in the shade. A Norwegian forest cat weighing twenty-five pounds could only be described as overweight, while a Maine coon, with its strong, muscular physique, can easily tip the scales at more than twenty-two pounds in fine shape.

Beware, however, of an excessively heavy Maine coon. Too much weight is harmful to bones, ligaments, and tendons. Unfortunately, hip dysplasia, typically a canine disease, also occurs in these large felines. For a predator that likes to keep on the move, climbing tall trees and performing breathtaking jumps, a deformation of the hip joints could be fatal.

Coon Cat?

There has been much speculation about the name *Maine coon*. Because this cat originates from Maine, it is clear to see where the first part of the name comes from, but the word *coon* puzzles many people. Allegedly, *coon* was derived from *raccoon*, so the cat was probably given this name due to the tail, which resembles a raccoon tail, as well as a reference to the sassy raccoon-like nature of this cat.

Simple and Straightforward

Anyone who has a Maine coon to call his own will know exactly why this breed, whose origins can be traced back to the mid-nineteenth century, is so incredibly popular. These fuzzy four-legged friends have a charming, uncomplicated character, and best of all, they are very easy to care for.

Although they are undoubtedly closely related to wildcats, they have proved themselves to be cuddly, loving family members that love affectionate pats and cozying up on the couch for hours. Maine coons are not as talkative as Oriental breeds and not as excitable as the more slender-built breeds; their nature is mainly balanced and peaceful with a few regular bursts of energy thrown in for good measure.

Feline Friends

Because Maine coons are a sociable breed through and through, you should not prevent them from having contact with other animals. It would be ideal to get two kittens so they can grow up together. Two or three cats together do not tend to get bored easily. If you are out a lot, they will have each other for company, and you will not have to worry about your pet being lonely. If a Maine coon is left alone for too long, his dreary, daily routine will quickly cause him to become very bored and introverted.

Fresh Air

If you have your heart set on a Maine coon, you will need to provide him with plenty of opportunities to roam around in the fresh air. These nature-loving cats appreciate outdoor trips in their enclosures and endless hours observing birds or chasing after butterflies.

If you have no way of providing your Maine coon with an outdoor enclosure, you could equip your balcony with a cat safety net to allow your pet to sit and purr in the sunshine. Safety nets are available on some online stores, and the latest designs are very easy to set up.

Norwegian Forest Cat

Build: large

Head: triangular; long, straight, sweeping profile; ears framed with fur

Eyes: large, oval, slightly slanted

Body: strong, elongated; large bones; long legs; hind legs longer than front legs; tufts of fur between the toes

Tail: long, bushy

Coat: medium length; woolly undercoat; water-repellent outercoat on flanks and back; long, dense, glossy beard and whiskers; chest has "shirtfront" appearance; ruff and "trousers"

Colors: all colors except colorpoint, chocolate, lilac, cinnamon, and fawn

This cat has a Nordic charm, with lynx-like tufts of fur on the tips of the ears.

The trademarks of the Norwegian forest cat include tufts of fur on the tips of the ears, a lion-like ruff, a gloriously fluffy tail, and cuddly "trousers" on the hind legs. These charming cats from the Far North are not quite as large as the Maine coons, but they are impressive nevertheless. Their medium-length, water-resistant outercoat and the dense undercoat give the impression of a much larger cat. The underside of the paws are also adorned with long tufts of hair—the so-called snowshoes. They prevent the cat from sinking into fresh powder snow.

As descendants of feral cats, Norwegian forest cats are very adaptable. Although their ancestors lived for many centuries on Scandinavian farms as part wildcat, this cuddly cat soon became used to humans. Provide him with a durable scratching post, toys, human affection, at least one other cat of the same breed, and a balanced diet.

Balconies and secure outdoor enclosures will be much appreciated by your cat. Owners who allow their Norwegian forest cats plenty of fun in the fresh air will find that this robust house pet has the courage of a lion. No weather is too cold for him because his oily guard hairs protect his body against moisture and the dense undercoat keeps this sturdy cat wonderfully warm.

Action, Please!

Norwegian forest cats are sociable animals. They love to mingle with others of the same breed. This spirited cat hates being left alone, and it is not advisable to leave your Norwegian forest cat on his own all day while you are at school. However, even if several animals live together, you will need to keep an eye on them to make sure they all get along well.

Meeting people is an important aspect of the Norwegian forest cat's lifestyle: these lovable cats from northern climates love the company of their humans and feel like a true member of the family. They want to participate in daily life in the household. Norwegian forest cats are interested in everything going on around them.

Well Adapted

This nineteenth-century breed is a masterpiece of evolution. Over time, their bodies have adapted to the ever-changing subarctic climate in the Scandinavian forests. The Norwegian winter is ice cold, and the summer is hot. This climatic roller coaster demands adaptability from the animal kingdom.

The Norwegian forest cat has passed this task with flying colors; in the winter, it is kept warm with the help of a magnificent fur coat. The thick undercoat protects the cat from the freezing temperatures, and the outercoat is waterproof so the wind and rain are kept away from the skin. The ears are decorated with lush tufts of fur to prevent them from getting too cold, and the tufts of fur between the toes help the cat to walk on snow.

Origin

The origin of this high-spirited bundle of energy from the cold forests of Norway is legendary. The story goes that the Norse god Thor tried to lift up a Norwegian forest cat, but it was simply too big and heavy. Also, the blonde goddess Freyja knew the treasured strength of this cat; according to the Scandinavian myth, these powerful cats pulled her sleigh through the forest.

A male named Pan's Truls was the sponsor for the first breeding standard, which was created in 1972. FIFe officially recognized the breed in 1976 and CFA in 1993.

Ragdoll

Build: large, strong

Head: medium size, broad; modified wedge shape; pronounced cheekbones; medium-size nose

Eyes: large, oval, blue

Body: elongated, muscular; broad chest; moderate bone size; medium-length legs; hind legs longer than front legs

Tail: long and furry, bushy

Coat: medium length, dense; soft, silky texture; long at the neck, short on the face

Colors: patterns: bicolor, colorpoint, mitted (white paws); **colors:** seal, blue, chocolate, lilac, red, cream

A blue-eyed beauty

For a long time, ragdolls were one of the more controversial American cat breeds, and they still have a reputation that lacks any real substance. Alarmingly, many cat lovers believe that ragdolls cannot feel pain, which, of course, is complete nonsense. Whether due to the much-debated recognition of the breed or its alleged magical powers, the ragdoll became caught up in the cross fire of criticism. Eventually, however, the waves of excitement died down. Also, there were longtime disputes between the creator of the breed, Ann Baker, and the ever-growing number of ragdoll breeders, but breeders are now in agreement: ragdolls are nothing more than just ordinary cats.

Stories of analgesia (insensibility to pain) and the unusual qualities of ragdolls have cursed this breed since it first began. Ragdolls originated in Riverside, California. In the 1960s, Ann Baker mated a white Angora-type cat with a male Birman cat. The result of this mating was the beginning of the ragdoll breed.

The Accident

What is so special about these kittens? Nothing really, apart from their gentle nature and astonishing beauty. However, the rumors began after the mother of the kittens, named Josephine, was in a car accident a month before she was due to give birth to her litter. It was a miracle that she survived, and consequently, she was said to have magical powers! Ann Baker claimed that Josephine was completely insensitive to pain and despite being thrown around like a ragdoll during the accident, she still survived. The American breeder went on to claim that Josephine had passed these magical properties on to her kittens. Of course, from a scientific point of view, this is not true.

The Struggle for Recognition

The ragdoll breed is now recognized in the United States by nearly all cat associations. But it was a long time before this happened. Birman breeders were highly critical of this new breed because they saw it as a poor imitation of the Birman. The application for recognition was rejected again and again because the organizations questioned the genetic purity of the ragdoll.

Nature

Ragdolls love to be people and hate to be left alone. Most cats of this breed are highly sociable and easygoing. Ragdolls also tend to fit into an existing family of cats very well, provided the other members of the cat group are tolerant of the newcomer. One continues to hear rumors that ragdolls are limp, slow, and uninteresting. Anyone who has seen one of these beautiful cats in action will know that this is not true. These attractive and fairly temperamental semilonghair cats are open minded and very interested in their environment. Ragdolls, which take four years to completely mature, are very curious, playful, and resourceful.

Colorful Cats

Ragdolls come in three varieties: colorpoint, mitted, and bicolor. In addition, there are six colors: seal, blue, chocolate, lilac, red, and cream. Throw in the tortie, tabby, and tortie-tabby patterns, and you have a number of looks

to choose from. These large, solidly built cats with muscular, elongated bodies have an incomparable charm of their own.

Birman

Build: medium size, strong

Head: neither too round nor too pointed

Eyes: almond shaped, slightly slanted, blue

Body: moderately sized, slightly elongated

Tail: medium length, furry, feathery

Coat: medium length; silky in texture; little undercoat

Color: lightly colored body (cream) with warm gold color on the back; rest of coat is same as colorpoint cats, but with four white paws; **points:** fur on face, ears, tail, and legs is darker in contrast to body color

This cat has eyes as blue as a mountain lake.

The Birman is said to have a high addiction factor. In fact, very few can resist the intoxicating beauty of the Birman cat. The Birman breed was officially recognized in France in 1925 and by the Cat Fanciers' Association in 1967. They are known for their particularly deep and comforting purr. Their meow is a sweet cooing sound that really tugs on your heartstrings. Their ability to charm and endear themselves to their people is an art unparalleled by any other breed. Birmans win over their owners with their calm temperaments. They are never over the top. Fans of this breed affirm that these cuddly furballs are highly intelligent. Some Birmans can open doors and even retrieve the phone from its holder when it rings! This cat can learn plenty of tricks and is always up for a challenge!

Origin

Many myths and legends surround the origin of these blue-eyed beauties. Whether they originated from the Asian mountains or not is beside the point. What is known for certain is that the beautiful Birman breed originated from a cross between bicolor long-haired cats and Siamese cats. Before World War II, a large number of these Birmans were crossed with Angora cat breeds. After the war, there was not as much breeding stock available, so other breeds were used instead, presumably Siamese and Balinese, possibly also Persian and domestic cats. In the mid-1950s, the breed was stabilized in France and a pair were exported to England, where, eleven years later, in 1966, the breed was officially recognized. In 1959, the breed was first imported into the United States.

Playful Yet Well Behaved

The unique, gentle nature of this breed means it is easy to train. The Birmans are people pleasers; it is not just this cat's beautiful coat you will fall in love with. She quickly understands which of her behaviors is not appreciated by her humans, making her a well-behaved cat too.

Playful by nature, Birmans show incredible enthusiasm for all sorts of objects around the home. Has her beloved human forgotten to buy her a new mouse toy? No problem—the crumpled envelope in the trash will do just as well and be tirelessly patted around the room.

Child Friendly

Most Birmans have a fondness for children, and their tolerance is something to behold when faced with lively two-legged playmates, any awkward movements or clumsiness is overlooked. Birmans that have grown up with children are particularly tolerant, but even if this is not the case, the Birman breed can quickly become used to children.

The More the Merrier

One Birman is great; two or three are even better! Happiness is guaranteed if an owner has two or three of these fluffy blue-eyed kitty cats. No human can replace a Birman's very own cat buddy that will give her a gentle lick behind the ears or snuggle with her. An uncomplicated nature makes the Birman an ideal breed for the elderly or large families. The quiet and adaptable Birman will easily fit into any lifestyle.

Siberian Forest Cat

Build: medium to large

Head: short, broad, rounded contours

Eyes: large, slightly oval, slightly slanted

Body: firm, muscular; medium-length muscular legs; large, round paws; tufts of fur between the toes

Tail: bushy

Coat: medium length, flowing, water-repellent overcoat; soft, dense undercoat; top layer of fur on back, flanks, and upper side of tail is dense and glossy; undercoat on underside of body and hind legs; long fur on the neck, chest, legs, and tail

Colors: all colors except chocolate, lilac, fawn, and cinnamon and variations on these colors

Meet the fluffy charmer from the cold East.

Forest cat breeds have experienced a huge surge in popularity in the last few years. Maine coons and Norwegians have long since conquered hearts with their medium-length fur coats, the lion-like ruffled collars, and extra-furry legs. These friendly, peaceful cats are, along with Persians, among the most popular pedigrees.

The Siberian belongs to this group of forest cats; however, it is less well known than its counterparts from Scandinavia and the United States. For many centuries, the Siberian cat was only known in his homelands of Russia and the Ukraine. In Russia, this breed was a much-treasured mouser and was admired more for his mouse-catching skills than his beauty.

It is said that Siberian cats are down to earth, and there appears to be more than a grain of truth in this claim. This medium-to-large-sized cat is not only bright and imaginative, he accepts his human family members just as they are.

As long as these cats have the opportunity for the occasional downtime and are able to eat their meals undisturbed, they are quite content to live in noisy households. They tolerate children, dogs, rabbits, and guinea pigs as well.

If their character had to be summed up in three words, they would be energetic, greedy, and chatty!

Origin

The Siberian cat is a typical example of the evolutionary wildlife of Russia and the Ukraine. The beautiful semilonghair cat has a dense, water-repellent coat, which protects his body effectively against cold and wet weather. This breed is also known for its robust health. The Siberian is the product of many centuries of natural selection.

The First Siberian Cats

The Siberian breed has been around for at least one thousand years. They were first mentioned in a book published in 1889 titled *Our Cats and All About Them* by Harrison Weir, an English artist known as the "father of the cat fancy." When the first Siberian cats actually arrived in Europe is debatable. There are several different written reports that are all within the realm of possibility; any one of these reports could be correct.

Supposedly, the first Siberian cats arrived in the West toward the end of the nineteenth century. At that time, the cats were known as Russian long-haired cats. In Great Britain, apparently, some of these cats were labeled as an unknown breed. The cats were said to have been mated with Angoras and Persians, which meant that the original phenotype, or physical appearance, of the Siberian cat was doomed. The growing popularity of Persians contributed to the downfall of this breed, and these four-legged beauties from Russia and the Ukraine fell into oblivion at the beginning of the twentieth century. FIFe did not recognize the breed until 1997.

The Siberian was imported into the United States in 1990 and accepted by the Cat Fanciers' Association ten years later. Although Siberians are a popular breed, they are very rare in the United States, so if you have your heart set on one of these beautiful cats, expect to be put on a waiting list!

Neva Masquerade

Build: medium, strong

Head: small, blunt, triangular; domed forehead; broad nose; strong, solid cheeks; pronounced chin

Eyes: large, slightly oval, blue

Body: elongated, with a short, strong neck; medium-length strong legs; large, round, strong paws; tufts of fur between the toes

Tail: broad, strong at base

Coat: long at neck, chest, thighs, and tail; thick and glossy along the back; fine, soft fur on sides of body

Colors: colorpoint seal, blue, red, cream, seal/blue tortie, smoke, tabby, silver, and golden; any amount of white allowed; chocolate, lilac, fawn, and cinnamon colorpoints not allowed

Meet the masked cat from the Russian Neva River.

His slightly slanted blue eyes are indescribably expressive, and his shiny medium-length fur invites you to pet him. Very few can resist the Neva masquerade's charms.

Not only do these immensely beautiful cats have an endearing character and incredible adaptability, but there is also a peculiarity about this breed that is far more than just a wild exaggeration. The Neva is a four-legged gourmand that finds it difficult to saunter past a tempting treat without stealing it and chomping it down greedily!

The Cat From the River

This breed has not been given its own category by FIFe, rather it is part of the same breed as the colorpoint Siberian cat. As with many other cat breeds, there is a debate that rages on as to the true origin of these cats. Supposedly, there is documentation stating that forest cats with masked faces had been observed around the Russian Neva River, hence the name of the breed.

On the other hand, some are of the opinion that the Neva masquerade is not an independent breed but a mix of various cat breeds. Also, it is possible that the Neva was the result of matings between Siberians and Thai cats. This is not improbable as countless color markings have emerged from the crossing of many different breeds, for example the Tonkinese, which is the result of a mating between a Siamese and Burmese.

Long-Standing Recognition

In Russia, it seems that the subject of the origin of the Neva masquerade is not up for discussion. The breed has been officially recognized there since 1990, and in St. Petersburg, there is even a club dedicated to this breed that has written books on this beautiful blue-eyed forest cat.

The Russian breeding programs include matings between Neva and Siberian cats. In view of the limited gene pool, this approach appears unwise and not supported by all breeders; in fact, many refuse to acknowledge the Siberian-Neva matings. Nevas are bred to Siberian cat standards, and Neva offspring can be produced from the pairing of two Siberian cats that have Neva ancestors and have the masked features of a Neva cat.

Different Color Varieties

Siberian cats and Neva masquerades differ only in terms of their color variety. Neva cats have a masked face and are technically a color variant of the Siberian. Any worries about an increased susceptibility to disease are unfounded with this breed, so fans can breathe a sigh of relief: Nevas are as healthy as other forest cat breeds. As with all other masked cats, they share the characteristic of being born with white fur and develop markings and a variety of fur colors during the first few weeks of life. These markings show how the colorpoint gene is related to a cat's body temperature. The cat's extremities (tail, legs, ears, feet, and face) are slightly cooler than the rest of the body, and so the fur on these parts is darker. According to the breed standard, these cats should have bright blue eyes, slightly lighter than the norm, but both eyes should be of the same color. A strong blue color is preferred—a typical characteristic of the masked cat. The Neva masquerade, just like the ragdoll, comes in patterned varieties: colorpoint, mitted, and bicolor. This enchanting breed can be admired in many varied coat colors.

Turkish Angora

Build: medium

Head: small to medium in size, wedge shaped

Eyes: large, almond shaped, slightly slanted

Body: fine bone structure; hind legs slightly longer than front legs

Tail: long and pointed, tapering, broad at the base, narrow at the end, fluffy

Coat: medium length on body; long, fine, silky fur on ruff; no undercoat

Color: all colors are permitted, including all varieties with white, with the exception of pointed patterns and chocolate, lilac, cinnamon, and fawn

A cat with soft, silky fur

When a peaceful Turkish Angora wraps his bushy tail around his front legs in a sweeping motion and then elegantly grooms his paw with his little pink tongue, you would think you were watching a real-life cat sculpture! An animal as beautiful as this could only have been created by an artist. It is rumored that Turkish Angora cats are the oldest breed in the world, and some people claim to be able to see the origin of all, or nearly all, semilonghair cats in this ancient breed. As lovely as this claim may be, it is rather difficult to prove. How much these modern beauties resemble their ancestors of the past few centuries we will probably never know. However, the history of the Turkish Angora is very interesting—the story began a long time ago . . .

A Turkish Gift

Let us travel back in time to the sixteenth century, when French and English commercial travelers returned home on ships carrying some of these charming, small, white creatures with them. Over time, they managed to spread as far as Asia Minor. These noble cats were seen as an ideal gift for a loved one back home and, in fact, they were the inspiration for many artists' paintings. Back then, pampered nobility had a fondness for Oriental-style furnishings and these cats were seen as an ideal addition to the household. Many paintings depict European leaders being presented with white Turkish cats as so-called luxury gifts. These lovely felines were owned by the richest people in Europe, but over the next century, they also stole the hearts of ordinary citizens. Around the end of the nineteenth century, these semilonghair cats were allegedly kept as pets in the homes of the middle classes, who also had a great interest in other long-haired breeds from Asia and Russia. Presumably, this was when excessive matings between individual breeds took place, which somehow led to the beginning of the Persian breed; this breed was known as the Angora, rather than Persian as it is known today. An interesting tidbit: According to legend, Mustafa Kemal Atatürk (1881–1938), the founder and first president of the Republic of Turkey, shall one day be reborn as a Turkish Angora cat.

In the Zoo

In the early 1960s, Turkey went through a period of great social unrest. This meant that the number of purebred Turkish Angoras dropped dangerously low, and the ancient breed was threatened with extinction. Turkish people did not want this to happen and attempted to preserve the breed by keeping a number of Angoras in zoos in Ankara and Istan as part of a selective breeding program for the future. Together with the United States, where some of these valuable breeding cats were exported, the Turkish Angora was saved from extinction. Even today, it is possible to admire Turkish Angora cats in Ankara Zoo.

Turkish and American Cats

The Turkish Angora cats in their home country and the Turkish Angora breed from the United States are actually very different. By the beginning of the 1990s, these pedigrees from the United States had become very long legged and

slender with dainty paws, and European breeders enviously admired their pretty faces with modified wedge-shaped heads and large ears.

Meanwhile, the European Angoras continue to have a loyal following, and any cat fan with little patience for grooming will be delighted to hear that not only is the fur of the Turkish Angora very beautiful, but it also requires very little care. Their medium-length coats are shorter in summer than in winter, and the fur has no undercoat, which is why it does not tend to mat.

Turkish Van

Build: medium to large

Head: short head; blunted triangle shape

Eyes: oval, slanted, large; light to dark amber, orange, blue, or two different-colored eyes

Body: muscular; strong bones

Tail: medium length, fluffy

Coat: chalk white, no yellow tinge; silky; no undercoat; short in summer, dense in winter

Color: colored tail, "butterfly" on head with white stripe running through middle, a few spots of color on the body are permitted

This cat loves swimming!

Turkish Vans are one of the rarest breeds around. This is surprising, for the whitewashed cat with the butterfly on her head is certainly not lacking in charm. One would have thought they could easily be as popular as Norwegian forest cats or Maine coons.

It is believed that Turkish Vans were a naturally occurring breed originating from Lake Van in Turkey. The climate in southeastern Anatolia, the peninsula comprising the Asian part of Turkey, is harsh: scorching hot summers alternate with icy cold winters. The Turkish Van had to adapt to extreme climates in order to survive. In the summer, this Turkish cat has a lighter, relatively short fur coat, which is dense enough to protect her body from intense solar radiation, but not as lush as the thick winter coat, which keeps the Turkish Van wrapped up, cozy, and warm, even in the hardest frost.

Fishing

There is only one type of fish living in the harsh, salty waters of Lake Van—the pearl mullet or Van fish—once the favorite food of the Turkish Van. Reportedly, these skillful hunters were particularly fond of fishing from the freshwater inflows, and their slippery prey met all their nutritional requirements. This hunting practice could be an explanation for this cat's great fondness for getting wet. This, of course, is not typical feline behavior as most cats will do anything to avoid getting wet! Although most modern Van cats are not afraid of water, they do not tend to go out of their way to find it.

A Souvenir Photo Journey

The discovery of this "merry sea-cat" occurred quite by chance. Two English travelers, Laura Lushington and Sonia Halliday, went on a photographic journey in Turkey in order to investigate the origins of the Turkish Angora. However, instead of encountering the mysterious ancestor, they found a white cat with silky fur, adorned with deep red markings on her head and tail. The women were astonished because these beautiful cats were quite different from what they had been expecting to find. Furthermore, some of these cats lived in the wild and some were also privately owned, as opposed to the Turkish Angoras, which were selectively bred in the zoo in Ankara.

The Turkish locals befriended these two English women and gave the charming travelers a pair of cats, which were directly imported to England without delay. In 1955, these two cats were the foundation for the Turkish Van breed that is known worldwide today and thus enjoy a legendary reputation.

A Groundbreaking Success

The real boom was during the mid-1970s. In 1969, the Governing Council of the Cat Fancy (GCCF), the major cat breed association in the United Kingdom, officially recognized the auburn and white Turkish Van, and FIFe followed three years later. In 1986 came recognition of the cream variants and since 1998, all other color varieties were recognized.

Independently of one another, Denmark, Holland, Switzerland, Sweden, and the United States imported the Van cats and established breeding in these countries. The first examples of these cats reached Germany in the mid-1980s.

However, a debate broke out on the colors. In England, Switzerland, and Germany, white-auburn and cream-white were still the only officially recognized Turkish Van colors. American, Dutch, Danish, and Swedish breeders were not discouraged by this breeding standard and imported different color variants, such as black-white and tabby-white from Turkey. This led to further color varieties, such as tortoiseshell-tabby and tortoiseshell-white.

Short-Haired Breeds and Somali

‹ **Burmese cats are known to be affectionate representatives of the shorthair breeds.**

› **Shorthairs have a very straightforward beauty regime.**

Short-haired breeds and Somali? At first glance, FIFe's category III of the cat breeds is somewhat confusing. After all, Somalis are the semilonghair relatives of the Abyssinian. So what do they have in common with their short-haired relatives? Indeed, there is a good reason behind this decision by the FIFe; the International Federation has placed the Somali in this category to highlight the relationship between the semilonghair Somali and the short-haired Abyssinian. However, independent cat associations usually place Somalis in the semilonghair category. This is useful to know, just in case you go to a cat breed show and are looking for Somalis in particular.

› Exotic Breed

Besides the Kurilian bobtail, Somalis are the only cats that have a special coat-length status within category III. All other breeds are short haired, though they do not all have the same tail length.

The short-haired breeds include not just British classics, such as the shorthair, Abyssinian, Russian blue, and Burmese, but also the more or less tailless companions: the Kurilian bobtail shorthair, Kurilian bobtail longhair, Manx cat, and Japanese bobtail. There is another cat in this category that is quite unlike the others—the mysterious sphynx. This delicate creature has no fur—at most a short, soft down—and a varying amount of wrinkles. This cat breed is not as popular in general, but anyone who has had the opportunity to hold one of these cats will be surprised at how charming and lovable these naked creatures are.

While on the subject of fur, the fur varieties of the rex group, consisting of the Cornish rex, German rex, and Devon rex, are very unusual. Their fur is made up of waves and curls. Cat lovers say they are quite alien compared to most cats, due to their unusual appearance, and

Abyssinian >38

Bengal >40

British Blue >48

British Shorthair >42

Burmese >44

Burmilla >46

Cornish Rex >50

Devon Rex >52

Egyptian Mau >54

European Shorthair >56

German Rex >58

Japanese Bobtail >74

Korat >60

Kurilian Bobtail >75

Manx> 75

Ocicat >62

Russian Blue >64

Snowshoe >66

Sokoke >68

Somali >70

Sphynx >72

bring something very different to this category. Category III is the largest and most varied of the four FIFe divisions, which makes for a lot of surprises.

> Known to All

If one studies individual breeds in more detail, it is clear that the popularity of each breed varies immensely. Without question, one of the most popular and well-known breeds is the British shorthair, which includes the blue varieties, also known as the Carthusian in some circles. The pure Carthusians are called the Chartreux, but they are so rare that a Carthusian enthusiast is not likely

to come across one. Many people who talk about the Carthusian cat are usually referring to the blue British shorthair. There is a section in this book dedicated to this smiling beauty. Burmese cats have become increasingly popular just as the Bengal and Abyssinian cats and ocicats and Russian blues are slowly becoming more common. Yet, none of these breeds are anywhere near as popular as the short-haired British breeds.

> Rarities

British shorthairs are very well known, compared to the other representatives of category III, which are relatively rare. Burmillas, Sokoke cats, and snowshoe cats are especially rare. If you are looking for a Burmilla, you would most likely find it in one of the Nordic countries or in Australia where they are bred more commonly. Most Sokoke cats are probably to be found romping through their local African rain forests, and snowshoe cats are only slightly more numerous in the United States.

Rex cats and bald cat breeds remain status symbols for the wealthy and those who want something out of the ordinary. And while we are on the subject, breeding of the European shorthair has practically come to a standstill. Too boring? Too mundane? Are there no longer any buyers for these kittens? This threat to the good old domestic cat is not to be underestimated. The best cats—often fine examples of the breed standard— are usually kept as family cats and therefore neutered, and the not-so-great examples are often unwanted and breed prolifically. If nothing is done to help the European shorthair breed, it faces a very uncertain future. That would be a shame because these cats have superior health, longevity, and an uncomplicated nature.

Abyssinian

Build: medium

Head: wedge shaped; broad forehead; graceful contours

Eyes: large, almond shaped, wide set, brightly colored; amber, green, or yellow; color is pure, clear, and intense; accentuated by fine dark lines; encircled by light-colored area

Body: medium length, strong, sleek, muscular

Tail: long, tapering, broad at the base

Coat: short, glossy, dense, lies flat against body

Color: two or three color bands on each hair with dark hair on tips preferred; ruddy (reddish brown) with black ticking, blue gray with dark blue gray ticking, sorrel (copper) with chocolate brown ticking, beige with cream ticking; silver varieties with black, blue gray, ruddy, or cream ticking

This cat is clever, canny, and always on the move!

The ticked fur is the unmistakable hallmark of an Abyssinian. Strictly speaking, this type of fur is known as ticked tabby, which refers to the striped banding of color on each strand of hair and is one of the official patterned markings. More cats have ticked fur than solid-colored fur, and in most of them, the ticked fur alternates with the solid color to create various different patterns, which is called "tabby."

The tabby pattern is determined by the tabby gene; the ticked hairs alternate with stripes, blotches, or spots of hairs with solid color. The commonly recognized types of tabby patterns have the following names: mackerel, classic, ticked, and spotted. For the four breeds—the Abyssinian and his relatives, the Singapura, Somali, and Ceylon—the ticked fur has been created by targeted breeding and is not the same as the Siamese, Persian, and British shorthair fur. These breeds also have ticked fur, but in different varieties. The agouti gene is responsible for ticked fur; each individual hair has bands of light and heavy pigmentation.

It is believed that the ticked tabby pattern originated from the Abyssinian cat breed. Or maybe those cats worshipped by the ancient Egyptians, which were most definitely wildcats, played a role? The concept of ticking was first mentioned in Europe in a reference to rabbit fur. Cat lovers first became aware of it in chinchilla cats and silver-shaded cats. The color and appearance of the fur tips, however, varied considerably from Abyssinian ticking.

Although there is no question that breeding of Abyssinian cats began in England, no one is completely certain where the first cats with ticking came from. There are various claims that the ancestors of the "Aby" were North African cats that were imported to England in the nineteenth century, and it is thought they were probably originally from Egypt.

Wild Coloring

The agouti gene is what gives a cat his wild coloring and can be seen on wild animals, such as deer and foxes as well as rabbits and guinea pigs.

On some cats, the ticking is strong and covers up any markings. However, many generations of pure ticking are needed for a cat to eventually have stripes. Consider the fact that the early examples of the Abyssinian breed had yellow gray banding on grayish beige background fur and had irregular stripes. The genetics of ticking are very complex.

A Ball of Energy

The wildcat-like appearance of this ticked beauty is not entirely misleading. Abyssinians are very fond of their freedom and have a confident nature. They are very active—walking, running, and jumping around tirelessly. Owners of this breed should give these cats something to climb on, or else they will most likely climb the curtains, cabinets, leather furniture, or floor lamps!

The nature of the Abyssinian differs from that of a wildcat because they seek out human company and love to be the center of attention. These little tigers are not happy when left alone and love to be part of a family. Their social behavior is so strongly pronounced that they generally fit in well into an already established cat population or in a household with dogs, though you should keep an eye out for this cat's constant attempts to be the boss. Caution: These willful cats will try to manipulate their two-legged friends. Abyssinians seem to instinctively know how to get around humans and force them into submission!

Bengal

Build: lithe, muscular, wildcat build

Head: broad, wedge shaped; round contours

Eyes: large, oval, slightly almond shaped

Body: long, strong, medium sized, robust, not delicate, very muscular

Tail: thick, tapering to the tip, rounded at tip, medium length

Coat: short to medium length, dense, lush; unusually soft texture

Color: brown (black) spotted, brown (black) marbled, seal sepia/seal mink spotted, seal sepia/ seal mink marbled

A jungle kitty for your living room!

"Curiosity killed the cat!" is a saying that hopefully will not apply to your Bengal. This beautiful cat is extremely curious by nature and has a tendency to put his pretty little nose where it does not belong! Fortunately, his curiosity is balanced with a large dose of intelligence and a strong character. These four-legged friends, formally known as leopardettes, have a fine instinct for danger and will retreat if they have to, no matter how curious they feel.

The name leopardette was used in the early days to refer to this relatively new breed. Breeder objectives varied enormously in terms of physical appearance: some had the aim of emulating leopards and ocelots, while others dreamed of a newer version of the Asian leopard cat, a small wildcat species, which is closer to how this breed eventually turned out.

Apart from exploring in order to satisfy their curiosity, these cats also enjoy cuddling and snoozing. However, not all Bengal owners are treated to this pleasure. Animals that are bred with barely any human contact are not very affectionate. Some display aggressiveness, severe anxiety, and a number of other problematic behaviors due to the way they have been bred; none of these are qualities of a lovable pet.

Even more scandalous is that some breeders think nothing of illegally importing Asian leopard cats. These exotic rarities are in high demand, even though the means of coming by these cats are not approved of by cat fans.

The Beginning of the Breed

Jean Mill, a geneticist and pioneer of the Bengal breed, began the first breeding program in 1963 in the United States, and she rigorously followed the breeding objectives. Mill, who at that time lived with her husband and daughter on a ranch in Arizona, bought a female Asian leopard cat, which was easier to acquire at the time, and bred this cat with her black domestic cat. This mating is officially considered the first intentional cross between a wildcat and domestic cat. Later, Mill crossed Egyptian Maus, spotted Abyssinians, Oriental shorthairs, and American shorthairs with leopard cats to create an affectionate pet with a wildcat appearance.

The mating of wild and domestic cats was unfortunately not as easy as one might suppose. Although Asian leopard cats and domestic cats each have thirty-eight chromosomes, different species cannot be crossbred successfully unless they are very closely related. As a result, the first hybrids were not domesticated and were also sterile.

Fancy Spots

The breeders searched for alternatives to increase the Bengal gene pool and turned their attention to the Egyptian Mau. The physique and of course the ticked fur met the criteria of the Bengal breeders. The same was true for the robust health and resilience of the Egyptian Mau, which was initially an issue for Bengal breeders. Today, the breed is well established in so far that it is no longer necessary to introduce any more crossbreeding.

Wildcat

Bengals look like wild, primal animals. Their lithe, medium-length bodies are impressively muscular. Although the breed is extraordinarily elegant, the robust bones mean they are very strong cats. These cats look similar to

small African leopards and ocelots. The friendly Bengal's personality, however, differs significantly from his wild relatives, which is fortunate; otherwise, the breed would probably never have become a household pet.

British Shorthair

Build: rounded, cuddly, toy-like appearance

Head: round, solid; broad skull

Eyes: large, round, wide set

Body: muscular, stocky; broad chest and shoulders

Tail: short and thick

Coat: short, dense, does not lie flat; thick undercoat

Color: white, black, black tortoiseshell, blue, blue tortoiseshell, chocolate, chocolate tortoiseshell, lilac, lilac tortoiseshell, red, cream, cinnamon, cinnamon tortoiseshell, fawn, fawn tortoiseshell

All colors mentioned above plus white van, harlequin, bicolor; colorpoint in all of these colors (except white); smoke, silver shaded/shell, golden shaded/shell, silver tabby, golden tabby; van/harlequin smoke, bicolor smoke, van/harlequin tabby, bicolor tabby, bicolor silver tabby, van/harlequin silver tabby, tabby point

Meet the doll-faced cat from the River Thames.

Cute, doll-like faces and vast expressive eyes are contributing factors to the immense popularity of British shorthairs, also known as BSH. This is true not only for the beautiful blue version, which is also known under the name Carthusian, but also for the whole motley variety of colors of the British shorthair breed. The many fans of this lovely breed melt when the cute, little, bear-cub-like figure comes running on his clumsy paws and happily pushes his head against outstretched hands for a much appreciated petting.

Hectic movements or psychological stress are not what this cat is about. Yet, this is not to imply this pretty British cat is in any way lazy or lethargic. They have the ability to become quite feisty, and once they do, there is no stopping them.

The origin of this cute and very confident, cuddly cat is in rainy Britain. This compactly built, short-haired breed originated from the Thames area at the end of the nineteenth century, and today his spell remains unbroken. A British shorthair won Best in Show at the world's first organized cat show, held in London's famous Crystal Palace in 1871. Is it any wonder that the BSH euphoria finally spilled across the English Channel? During the twentieth century, German and Dutch cat fans succumbed to this lovable breed and dedicated themselves to the task of carrying on the breed in Europe.

A Variety of Colors

The first specifically British-bred plushy cats had striped coats. This was followed by crossbreeding domestic cats and multicolored Russian beauties. Siamese cats also contributed to the spectacular expansion of the color palette. Pretty Angora cats brought to England were also added to the mix, so the precise origins of this attractive breed are difficult for experts to trace. Red, white, and cream were among the first colors produced by breeding experiments, and the new colors in all kinds of variations increased the popularity of the breed. Brindle characteristics were particularly applauded.

Persian Heritage

Persians, with their thick, luxurious coat of fur, made an active contribution to the establishment of the British shorthair breed. British breeders were very happy with the significantly improved coat quality thanks to the Persian gene, and participated in the battle against the unwanted longhair gene. In addition, the eye color is not always entirely as it should be according to the breeding standard, and that could ultimately be due to the legacy of crossbreeding with Persian cats. Incidentally, many breeders are now trying to rule out crossings with Persian cats so as not to compromise the unusual eye color of the British shorthair anymore. This is again at the expense of the fur quality, however. As is so often the case in cat breeding, the greater the challenge for the breeders, the louder the applause when these lofty goals are actually achieved.

Color and Character

Fans of the breed are convinced that the characteristics of each cat depend on its fur color. Despite his strikingly beautiful coat color, the British blue is said to be the most pigheaded out of any of the other colors, while the tabby cats are intelligent and patient. The silver varieties are rumored to be extraordinarily sensitive, while the tortoiseshell-colored beauties are said to be quite stubborn.

Burmese

Build: elegant, athletic

Head: short wedge shape, wide at cheekbones

Eyes: wide set, expressive, lively, bright; gold or yellow desirable

Body: medium length, muscular, compact

Tail: straight, medium length

Coat: very short, fine, silky, shiny; almost no undercoat

Color: brown, blue, blue tortoiseshell, chocolate, chocolate tortoiseshell, lilac, lilac tortoiseshell, red, cream, seal tortoiseshell; all colors brighter on the back and legs, paler on the underparts

This cat loves people!

Anyone who encounters a Burmese cat will find it hard to resist its charming nature. This open, friendly breed seeks out contact with people, and it is for good reason these cats are said to be as loyal and affectionate as any dog. Burmese cats are relatively unobtrusive, but they do like to be the center of attention. Their temperament is simply fantastic, and their ingenuity and intelligence never cease to amaze. Enthusiasm and a strong urge to be constantly on the move are other characteristics exclusive to this breed. If their people do not have time to play with them, they are just as happy to run around the house. Burmese cats love companionship, so it is ideal for them to be in contact with their own kind as much as possible.

However, it should be noted that Burmese cats are fairly dominant beings and tend to take over other cats in the household—they like to be the boss!

Where Do They Come From?

Burmese cats are from Southeast Asia and are closely related to the Siamese cat. Ancestors of the Burmese cat have been traced back to the fifteenth century, though their main area of distribution at the time was Thailand rather than Burma.

It is assumed that the slim build evolved as a response to the harsh climate and living conditions. As a result, many Oriental cat breeds reproduce prolifically: harsh living conditions result in high mortality. The more young produced, the greater the likelihood of survival of the species.

Along with Siamese, Burmese cats belong to the oldest Oriental breeds in Europe and, along with Persians and Siamese cats, are among the most popular breeds in Britain and the United States. However, their breeding history is still relatively young. The first Burmese cat was imported to America in 1930.

The First Blue Burmese Cat

The 1950s saw the arrival of the first ever blue Burmese cat. Toward the end of 1950, in the United States, the first chocolate-colored Burmese was bred. The beginning of the 1970s saw the addition of the lilac color, and even before this color was officially recognized, the colors red and cream were added to the breed. In the mid-seventies, these color varieties were

officially recognized. By the end of the 1970s, the four tortoiseshell colors had also been recognized. The Burmese breed now has ten beautiful color varieties, with solid colors being an example of good quality breeding. Along with England and the United States, Australia and New Zealand also have a high status for Burmese cat breeding. Many silver varieties originate from Australia and New Zealand. However, England is still regarded as the true country of origin of the Burmese breed.

Burmese color varieties are generally characterized by the fact that the fur on the underside of the body is paler than on the back and the legs. The markings on the face and ears are of a darker color than the rest of the body.

The People's Cat

Aside from the stunningly beautiful colors of the Burmese breed, it is the character of this breed that makes Burmese cats so irresistible. Also worth noting is its distinctive voice. The Burmese is an extremely talkative breed; it expresses its different moods using many tones and pitches. Apart from when the female is in heat, the Burmese cat's voice is pleasant and generally not perceived to be a nuisance in any way.

Stroking and cuddles are among the basic requirements of a Burmese cat. They seek out contact with their people and also their own kind. Groups of Burmese cats tend to snuggle close together and purr. Physical contact with their humans is of particular importance to this cat.

Burmilla

Build: elegant, medium sized

Head: short, blunt wedge shape; gently rounded contours; medium to large, wide-set ears that often sit forward on the head

Eyes: large, bright, expressive; green framed by black outline

Body: medium length, muscular; strong legs

Tail: straight, medium to long, slightly rounded tip

Coat: very short, fine, glossy, silky texture

Color: always silver shaded or silver shell

Group I: Non-Orange— black, blue, chocolate, lilac, cinnamon, fawn, silver/ golden shaded/shell

Group II: Orange—red, cream, tortoiseshell, silver/ golden shaded/shell

Meet the cat with elegant coloring as delicate as any watercolor painting.

The name Burmilla is a fusion of the words *Burmese* and *chinchilla,* and it is quite easy to see where this breed, with its silvery, shimmering fur, got its name. It all began in the 1980s and was the result of a random pairing that laid the foundations for a new era in cat breeding. A silver chinchilla male mated with a lilac Burmese female. Their offspring had captivating, shimmering silver fur. The quality of the breed and the pleasant nature of these small hybrids lead to further breeding attempts, resulting in the origin of the Burmilla breed. The adventure began when Miranda Bickford Smith bought a chinchilla cat named Jemari Sanquist for her husband. As already mentioned, the mating of the lilac Burmese female was purely accidental and had unpredictable consequences. A few weeks later, four black-shaded silver kittens appeared. Two of these kittens, Galatea and Gemma, were the starting point of the Burmilla breed.

Intoxicating Beauty

With only a small gene pool, the first years were very difficult. However, over time, more and more breeders became interested in the incredibly beautiful creation of this silver-coated cat. Well-known catteries let their purebred cats "go wild" and thus contributed to the expansion of the gene pool. The experiment was successful and, in 1983, the breed was rewarded with preliminary registration by the Cat Association of Britain (CA). Seven years later, when the CA became the first British cat association to be a member of FIFe, the official recognition of the breed came with a revised standard.

Burmilla breeding required breeders to have a good knowledge of genetics. Over time, thanks to this knowledge, the two breeds—Persian chinchilla and Burmese chinchilla, or Burmilla—became completely different from one another. Two recessive genes (those that are carried but not expressed) had to be eliminated in order to produce a pure Burmilla: first, the longhair gene of the Persian, and secondly, the non-agouti gene of the solid-colored Burmese. Five generations were needed to eliminate these genes and for the breed to acquire pedigree status. In order to achieve this, inbreeding could not be avoided.

Inbreeding

Many are critical of inbreeding; however, if done intelligently, it can be of use. "After matings between brothers, sons, and fathers with daughters, mothers, and sisters, from the filial generation (the generation resulting from a genetically controlled mating that is successive to the parental generation), kittens are produced with around 16 percent of the undesirable genes. The first generation is made up of animals which do not comply with the ideas of the breeders. In the second generation, there is a larger number of kittens which do not carry undesirable genes," explains the Danish breeder Bengt Aggersbol.

These undesirable genes have long since been overcome, but the popularity of these beautiful Burmillas is somewhat lacking in Europe, unlike in Australia, where there are plenty of interesting breeding programs taking place. Why Burmillas are not popular elsewhere remains an enigma, as it cannot be due to their lack of charm. They are elegant cats of medium size, with hind legs slightly longer than their front legs. It is not just their silky fur that makes them beautiful, but also their huge wide-set eyes, which give them a slightly mysterious expression. The eyes come in every shade of sparkling green; a clear bright green is the preferred shade. For cats under the age of two, a light yellow tinge is acceptable. Red, cream, and tortoiseshell Burmillas are also permitted to have amber eyes, according to the breed standard.

British Blue (Carthusian)

Build: large, heavy, solid

Head: round, solid, broad skull; strong chin; short, broad nose with a slight indentation (snub nose)

Eyes: large, round, open, wide set; copper colored or dark orange

Body: muscular, stocky; broad chest and shoulders; strong back

Tail: short and thick; slightly rounded tip

Coat: short, dense, does not lie flat; thick undercoat

Color: The color of each hair should be uniform to the root.

Meet the irresistibly cuddly blue "bear cub."

Many people will have heard of the Carthusian cat. Almost everyone is familiar with this beautiful blue cat breed, which, despite its imposing size, trots elegantly across the screen in countless television commercials. The blue bear, or the British blue, has won countless hearts in recent years. For many, they are the epitome of the ideal cat: impressive, beautiful, lovable, and cuddly. FIFe recognizes the Chartreux (pictured left) as a separate breed, described by some as the real Carthusian. However, Charteux cats are very rare and much less popular than the blue Britons.

As the name suggests, the British blue originated in England. It is estimated that these compactly built, short-haired cats were widely known and were bred for more than one hundred years. It did not take long for enthusiastic German and Dutch cat lovers to catch on. To continue the breed, they used the finest examples of these blue cats, as well as Persians from England.

These cats were crossed with Persians in order to give the breed a certain nobility and also to introduce the orange eye color. Nowadays, Persians are no longer crossed for the continuation of this breed, and some breeders will deny this was ever the case. However, it is difficult to ignore this historical fact when a breeder finds a long-haired British blue in his newborn litter!

This can happen if both parents carry the longhair gene of the Persian and the gene is passed on to their offspring. The breeder would not have any idea both parents carried the gene until the kittens were born. Although this feature has no health disadvantages, these long-haired kittens would obviously not be chosen to continue the British blue breed because this would threaten the coat texture according to the specific breed standard. The breed standard dictates that the coat should be short and dense. Due to the thick undercoat, the fur does not need to lie flat against the body but must be neat and tidy.

BSH or Chartreux?

If you are seriously interested in purchasing a Carthusian cat, you will notice straightaway that the whole thing is very confusing for regular cat owners. Cat lovers may admire the attractive blue coat and expressive, bright eyes. However, Carthusian cats (British shorthairs) and the blue Chartreux breed do have clear boundaries. The breeders emphasize the independence of the two breeds that also have specific pedigrees. The confusion began in 1967, when the FIFe put these two breeds under the same heading because of their obvious similarities. At this time, frequent matings between Chartreux and British shorthair cats actually occurred. Today, this is no longer allowed. In 1977, FIFe decided these breeds were in fact different from one another and provided pedigrees for the British blue, with the addition of the "Carthusian." In 1991, the separate section for the Carthusian breed was abolished and the official name for these blue cats became the British blue. However, this history refers exclusively to the FIFe. Numerous other cat associations refer to the British blue as Carthusians, while others use the term in reference to the Chartreux. The Chartreux has been labeled as an independent breed by FIFe, CFA, ACFA, and TICA.

Shape and Color

The physical characteristics of the British blue are much admired by cat lovers. The round, solid head with the remarkably wide skull; the short, wide snub nose with a gentle indentation; and strong chin give the British shorthair an imposing, doll-like appearance. The large, round, wide-open eyes stand out with their bright copper color or a beautiful dark orange and are exceptionally expressive. The small ears, slightly rounded at the tips, are wide set and frame the face of this enchanting cat.

Cornish Rex

Build: medium

Head: wedge-shaped skull; long, straight profile; flat forehead

Eyes: oval shaped, slanted

Body: elegant, slender, muscular, elongated

Tail: long

Coat: no topcoat; velvety soft, short, wavy fur; curly whiskers and eyebrows

Color: all colors and patterns

A strong personality with curly fur

At the beginning, it was nothing more than a spontaneous mutation that led to the emergence of the Cornish rex. The genetic characteristics expressed themselves in the form of pretty, curly fur, a phenomenon that, within a few years, was seen on several different cat breeds. While some breeders were not particularly interested in this funny little curly creature, breeders in England took it upon themselves to breed this cat prolifically. An efficient breeding program helped to establish the new breed. Over the next few decades, Cornish rexes became increasingly well known all over the world. They have curly or at least wavy fur and also have curly whiskers and eyebrows. The short, dense coat feels plushy and soft. This affectionate and extremely social character is usually found only in Britain. Not only is this an uncomplicated breed, it is also ideal for keeping as an indoor cat. The Cornish rex has an extraordinary expression, due in particular to its medium, oval-shaped eyes, which are a stunning shade of copper or amber.

A Resemblance to Siamese

Cornish rexes resemble Siamese cats, except that their fur is curly. Ideally, the coat should have short, successive waves, giving the effect of an even, all-over pattern. According to FIFe standards, all colors and patterns are recognized. The Cornish rex has the long-legged look of a Siamese, as well as the very long tail, which should be covered in plenty of curly fur.

Judges of cat shows pay particular attention not only to the fur of the Cornish rex, but also to the body shape. A medium, wedge-shaped head is desirable, and the head should be a third longer than it is wide. Bald spots or tails with no fur are not desirable.

Expertise Required

Successful Cornish rex breeders are highly regarded. Specific knowledge is required. For example, although rex kittens are born with attractive curls, they lose these curls temporarily. At about the age of three months, the waves and curls return. Larger kittens will be more affected by this transformation than their smaller and more delicate littermates.

Another characteristic of the breed is that these cats appreciate a warm environment. When it is cold and wet, no Cornish rex will voluntarily go outside. To make life a bit more pleasant for these curly four-legged creatures, it is a good idea to provide them with an additional heat source, under the cat bed for example. This is not a requirement for good health but it will definitely benefit the well-being of your kittens. The same applies for physical contact. Cornish rexes feel at their best when they are near their caregivers. Fans of the breed say that rexes are exceptionally intelligent. Anyone who underestimates this runs the risk of being manipulated! The curly Cornish rex understands his people very well and is extremely good at charming his owner and also his own kind. In a group of cats, the rex will happily take the lead.

Look to the Future

Although the relatively rare breed is growing in numbers, it does not have a huge fan base. "In some countries there are many different rexes, in other countries, only one type. In Germany, the popularity of the rex breed is on the increase. The breeders of this cat are very knowledgeable," said Anneliese Hackmann, president of the World Cat Federation.

All in all, things are looking up for the medium-sized Cornish rexes whose bodies are immensely strong and muscular yet slim. If you would like a cat that is extraordinary, you will find your perfect cat in this exceptionally lovable and affectionate, curly friend.

Devon Rex

Build: medium

Head: short and broad

Eyes: large, oval, wide set

Body: medium size, muscular; long tail

Coat: no topcoat; very short, fine, soft, wavy fur; whiskers and eyebrows are curly

Color: all colors and patterns

This rex breed has characteristically long hind legs.

A wavy coat; large, expressive eyes; and a short, wedge-shaped head are the unmistakable hallmarks of the Devon rex. You may have heard this somewhere before—this breed shares many similarities with the Cornish rex and the German rex. Sometimes described as a cuddly alien, there are not many breeds with which you can form such an immediate bond. Rexes are simply incredibly lovable four-legged charmers that are quite happy to live life as indoor pets.

The breed began by accident in the 1960s after a random pairing of stray cats in Devon, England. At the time, of course, its fur was nowhere near as curly as today; a genetic mutation somewhere down the line was responsible for the curly fur of this breed. Specialized breeding programs increased over the years in order to obtain the desired traits, but initially, various hurdles had to be overcome. In the past, unfortunately, there were many inbred diseases because serious errors were made while breeding these cats. Also, the coat quality left a lot to be desired. Over several decades, experienced breeders were able to weed out the mistakes made before and thanks to competent selection, no more errors were made. The fur quality of the Devon rex is now usually outstanding. There are varieties with white fur and golden eyes that are especially popular, although the Devon rex is available in all colors and patterns. The wide-set eyes are stunning due to their large size and lovely, clear color. The thick, curly whiskers and eyebrows give this extravagant beauty an extra-special flair.

Dachshund Legs

Devon rexes have a triangular head with a short nose and are usually not as curly as the German rex or the Cornish rex. They are somewhat stockier, and the positions of their legs resemble that of a dachshund. The length of the hind legs is emphasized; these long, strong legs are well suited to making large leaps. Judges devote special attention to the head, build, and character, as well as the fur. Allowances are made for different fur types. The breed should not have bald patches, but the fur should be very short, fine, and extremely soft. A full coat of fur is a definite preference, although many Devon rexes have a down on their tummies rather than fur.

Expressive

Most Devon rexes are very expressive with their affection. They are very loving and sociable, which is a characteristic that judges hold in high regard. Supposedly, these curly creatures are able to sense whether someone likes them or not. They share this ability with the sphynx cats, which also have plenty of intuition and common sense.

Devon rexes are not only good judges of character, but they are also full of surprises: "The most striking thing I ever saw in my life was an exhibitor at a cat show in Italy. He had seven Devon rexes clinging to him and hanging from his coat as he walked through admissions. He carefully removed all of the cats from his coat, and set them down in front of the vet to be examined," recalls Anneliese Hackmann.

Longevity

The cat expert is very impressed by rexes: "After Siamese, Orientals, Persians, Burmese, and also some British breeds, I can say that where health is concerned, the rex cats win hands down," says Hackmann. "Many of my cats have reached a grand old age—my Burmese cat was twenty years old. There are many factors which contribute to life expectancy. But it has been my experience that the smaller cats, the more delicate breeds, have a life expectancy which is just as high, and this is certainly the case for the rexes."

Egyptian Mau

Build: elegant

Head: slightly rounded wedge; pronounced cheekbones

Eyes: large, watchful, almond shaped, slightly slanted

Body: medium, muscular; loose fold of skin from flank to back knee

Tail: medium length, thick at base, moderately pointed at tip

Coat: medium length, lustrous; fur is silky and fine in the smoke variety and dense in the silver and bronze varieties; fur is fine and long enough for two or more bands of ticking; the lighter bands are separated by darker bands

Color: black smoke, black silver spotted, bronze spotted

The cat from ancient Egypt

Rare is the cat lover who can walk past an Egyptian Mau without a second glance. Clearly separated spots adorn the mid-length, shiny fur and are more than a little reminiscent of a wildcat. Whether the elegant fur is smoke, silver, or bronze, this proud cat always has a mysterious M marking on her forehead ("the mark of the scarab") and creates a storm of enthusiasm wherever she goes.

The Mau became a hand-tamed subspecies of the African wildcat, originating from the Ethiopian highlands. At least this was the conclusion the cat expert and Egyptologist Morrison Scott came to, after devoting himself to the intensive investigation of the more-than-two-thousand-year-old mummified cats.

We need to take quite a big step into the past to find the origins of these spotted gems. The exact historical development of the breed remains unconfirmed, but there are various hints in relevant literature that outline a few interesting ideas. The official version reports that a Russian princess discovered two beautiful Egyptian Maus on a trip to Italy and took these cats home with her. In 1953 and 1954, the first Egyptian Mau litters arrived. These spotted beauties went back to the Fatima Cattery belonging to the Russian princess and are seen as the beginning of the lineage.

Recently, this breed has been mated with representatives of the so-called Indian lineage, the aim of which is to give a better contrast and markings and improve the coat. This mating is also said to achieve a more striking head shape.

European Spotted Fever

In Europe, after World War II, things were not looking good for the Egyptian Mau breed. The astonishingly beautiful breed was considered virtually extinct, yet, as far as it was known, no one was attempting to breed these cats. However, the spotted beauty rose like a phoenix from the ashes.

Breeders from Switzerland, the Netherlands, and Italy imported American Maus from the original lineage. First, the Mau was recognized by independent cat associations, which were then followed by the FIFe. Finally, one could admire Egyptian Maus in European exhibitions. Their popularity grew, and German and French breeders also began to import cats from the original lineage of this breed from the United States.

Natural Breed

Because the gene pool of this extraordinary breed is still relatively small, Europe still imports Egyptian Maus from the United States today. Despite numerous loud protests, European breeders have also begun to breed from Indian lineage. This has led to a small group of committed Mau fans fighting for the purity of the breed. They coined the phrase "natural breed" because their breed comes from the first generation of Egyptian Maus and may not be bred with other breeds. Many breeders consider this pairing with Indian lineage as disadvantageous for the Mau breed.

Naturally Extreme

When asked to describe their cats, Egyptian Mau owners will rave about the nature of these active, colorful cats. It is said that these muscular felines have a distinctive individuality, insatiable curiosity, and an innate openness. Some say that ownership of these lovable cats with their blend of strength, substance, and grace has enhanced their lives tremedously.

The unusual character of the Egyptian Mau is alleged to have a tendency to extremes. When she opens her heart to her owner, she loves him mind, body, and soul. When a Mau spots something of interest to her, she is driven with zeal and a tenacious curiosity. This graceful, spotted cat is said to have been counted among one of Cleopatra's many passions.

European Shorthair

Build: medium

Head: large

Eyes: round, wide eyed

Body: robust, strong, muscular

Tail: medium length, thick at base

Coat: short, dense, springy, shiny

Color: white, black, blue, red, cream, black tortoiseshell, blue tortoiseshell, and all these colors in smoke, tabby, silver tabby, and van/harlequin/bicolor

The European shorthair is a natural breed.

This breed is the secret queen of neighborhood yards, sneaking around on soft, silent paws. Many consider these cats to be the natural representative of the motley cat world. They have an amazing robustness, longevity, and pronounced intelligence. Many claim that these domestic cats, in contrast to their blue-blooded relatives, the pedigree cats, are instinctively able to survive without human assistance.

One thing is undisputed: European shorthairs have a simple elegance and are perfectly capable of living without a fancy fluffy tail, unusual ears, or a dazzling leonine ruff. They spread charm everywhere they go and add a touch of wildness to the suburban yard. Somehow, millennia-old history radiates from the eyes of this domestic cat—the most perfectly designed natural predator. Her stalking skills are incomparable, the speed of her reactions cannot be imitated, and she has mastered the art of climbing the tallest trees around.

When Freedom Calls

Although there are vast differences, and perhaps it is not true of all these cats, they are undoubtedly known to love wandering through woodlands and meadows, and are freedom-loving, purring mousers. These cuddly pets do perfectly well without having trophies and praise heaped upon them; they appreciate their independence and have a seemingly limitless desire for freedom. All is fine in their world if they are allowed to leave the shelter of their home whenever the mood takes them; they love to roam freely in the wild and have exciting outdoor adventures.

Soft padded baskets and cuddly, homey naps on a satin pillow are not high on the priority list for these enterprising explorers. This cat derives far more pleasure from mysterious hideouts in the long grass or under dense bushes—there are far more interesting things to be observed there than from a bored glance at the floral pattern on the living room wallpaper.

A Masterpiece of Evolution

Cats are the incarnation of the perfect predator, a masterpiece of evolution, as portrayed on a daily basis by this domestic cat. Each individual fiber of her elegant body is designed to hunt. She uses her quick reactions and sharp canines to catch her prey.

Creeping, silent stalking, a short sprint, climbing, and jumping are the specialties of the family *Felidae*—but when you see her purring on the sofa, it is easy to forget she is a skilled hunter with deadly, razor-sharp teeth and needle-sharp claws.

The successful sprinter holds her prey in her mouth and grips it with her claws and fangs. The sharp canines penetrate the delicate vertebrae and can kill a mouse in seconds. Although cats can kill quickly, often a rodent will suffer before it is killed. This predator enjoys an extensive game, torturing her trophy for long moments before finally sinking her teeth into her helpless victim.

We Leave at Dawn

At dawn and dusk, house cats get to work. They stalk unsuspecting prey that leave the protection of their nests and come out of hiding to search for food.

These predators that hunt in the shadows are equipped with highly developed senses. They can see far better than humans, and their hearing tells them how far away another animal is from them.

German Rex

Build: medium

Head: rounded, with good width between the ears

Eyes: medium size, wide eyed, good distance from the nose line, bright color; eye color matches coat color

Body: medium size, strong, muscular

Tail: medium length, powerful base tapering slightly toward the tip, roundish tip, plenty of fur on tail

Coat: soft, velvety, short, plushy, wavy or curly

Color: all permitted, whiteness allowed in coat

The German answer to the Cornish rex and Devon rex

Rex fans describe the nature of their curly darlings as extremely friendly. These cuddly creatures are indoor cats that need lots of affection. Rexes are very sociable with people, and their playfulness and ingenuity are noteworthy. This little prankster invents a new trick just about every day. Acrobatic feats, daring jumps, and boisterously climbing the living room cabinets are among the favorite activities of the very curious German rex.

When greeting children and strangers, rexes are rarely shy. They behave confidently in even the most unfamiliar situations and always remain friendly. Dealing with other cats, however, is a different story: the German rex wants to be master of the house and is likely to assert his dominance over other cats. The hierarchy will be made clear without a great deal of fuss, meaning the other cat will know his place, but this could include a few swipes of the paw in the first instance.

Taking care of a German rex's coat is simple. His care regime requires nothing more than a daily stroke and a few cuddles. During shedding season, the amount of fur he sheds is moderate; you could rub his coat daily with a chamois leather to remove any loose fur.

Features

Most prospective rex owners are surprised when they see how small the rex is.

The curly fur typical of this breed is present in a newborn kitten but disappears shortly afterward. The disappearance of the curly coat is linked to the rapid weight gain of a young rex. The skin stretches so fast during the growing phase that the fur growth cannot keep up. After the first shedding, the wavy fur grows again but it can take up to two years before the curliness of the fur reaches its full potential.

Origin

Rex cats are not a result of intentional breeding. Worldwide, there have been many separate accounts over the years of domestic cats that had curly hair. Largely, however, these animals were not chosen for specific breeding. The curly fur gene responsible for rex fur is a recessive gene and is a spontaneous mutation that affects the appearance of a cat. Until specific inbreeding is undertaken to isolate the gene for curly fur, these cats remain in the minority.

In order to understand the origin of the German rex, we must go back to the first decades of the twentieth century. At this time, curly-haired cats were not called rexes. Rex was the name given by a British rabbit breeder in Cornwall who discovered a litter of ordinary domestic cats with curly fur. This was about 1950. However, it is undisputed that cats with curly fur were around long before this in Germany. In the early 1930s in East Prussia, there was a cat named Munk that quite clearly had the curly fur gene. Allegedly, Munk was the result of a mating between a Russian blue and a brown Angora cat. This cat is considered to be the oldest known example of a German rex. Since there was no specific further breeding, this particular line disappeared and was not experimented with again.

The next evidence for the existence of the German rex was in 1951. Dr. Rose Scheuer-Karpin discovered a curly cat on the site of the Berlin Hufeland Clinic. It was predicted that the curly descendants of this cat would make a splash with cat fans.

In Germany, the German rex breed had a small gene pool, which meant that the crossing of domestic cats was required. A Persian cat and a Devon rex were crossed to start off this breed.

Korat

Build: medium

Head: heart shaped when viewed from the front; very wide-set eyes

Eyes: almost too large for face, bright, expressive, wide eyed, round

Body: medium size, muscular, supple, powerful; arched back

Tail: medium length, strong at base, rounded and tapered tip

Coat: short to medium length, shiny and fine; lies flat against body

Color: silver blue only; silver fur tips, no shading or stripes

The Korat is a rare gem with a mysterious expression.

Korats are the rarest of the four blue breeds and in terms of popularity, they lag far behind the British blue, the increasingly popular Russian blue, and the Chartreux, which has made a comeback, particularly in France. In addition to their breathtaking beauty and lovable nature, they also have a very interesting past.

It is only in the United States and Canada that there is a Korat breeding scene to speak of. There are very few breeders of this picturesque feline in Europe.

Fur Made of Clouds and Silver

The lithe, muscular Korats are one of the oldest natural breeds around. They originate from beautiful Thailand, where their exceptional attractiveness was highly commended in the *Smud Khoi of Cats* manuscript during the Ayutthaya period (1350–1767). The name *Korat* appears to have originated from the Northern Thai Korat Province. Supposedly, in this region, there are more blue cats than in any other part of the country. King Rama V, who reigned during the nineteenth century and at the beginning of the twentieth century, allegedly asked about the origin of these cats and decided to call them Korat from that point on, as he was told they were from the Korat Province.

Appearance

The body of a Korat is not nearly as short as that of a Manx cat, but not as long as that of a Siamese. Observe the stunning blue beauty as she uses her medium-length, strong, slender legs to execute an enormous leap onto a high shelf. Allow yourself to be inspired by her large, round eyes, a charming and mysterious shade of golden green. Some American breeders refer to the expressive eye color of a Korat as a "traffic-light green" or "peridot green" in an attempt to describe the incredible luminosity of the Korat's eyes.

The eye color of this affectionate cat from Thailand is fully developed by the end of her second year of life, but she will have captured your heart long before this—and not just because her head shape actually resembles a small heart. Gently stroke the shiny, silver gray, short-to-medium length fur, and you will clearly be able to feel the muscular body underneath, due to the lack of undercoat. The tips of the fur have a magical silver shimmer and this is particularly noticeable on the body parts with very short fur (nose, ears, and paws). According to the FIFe standard, white tufts or patches are undesirable, as is the fur being any color other than silver blue.

A Successful Export From Thailand

After many centuries of delighting the Thai people, the first Korat cats reached the United States in 1959. Because the gene pool of the Korat breed was very small at the beginning, they were crossed with two blue point Siamese cats. Fortunately, more cats were soon imported from Thailand and this freshened up the available breeding stock, meaning no inbreeding was necessary. This was the beginning of an unstoppable career.

Ocicat

Build: muscular, not plump

Head: modified wedge shape; broad nose

Eyes: large, almond shaped, slightly slanted; all colors except blue

Body: elongated, strong, powerful; strong bones; wide chest

Tail: moderately long, slightly pointed, dark at tip

Coat: short, colored banding, smooth, close fitting, silky texture, glossy

Color: black (tawny), blue, chocolate, lavender, cinnamon, fawn, and silver spotted; clear, strong contrasting—lighter on the face, around the eyes, chin, and lower jaw; ticking: all hairs except the tail are banded; darker tipping on the spots, lighter tipping on the overall fur color

Meet this highly intelligent, rare breed.

Severely damp air, oppressive humidity, jungle vines, and the shrill cry of an exotic bird are parts of the true ambience for this muscular, speckled beauty as he stalks through the undergrowth with undeniable elegance. However, ocicats are much happier creeping around human dwellings in the urban jungle. As a matter of fact, this clever, cuddly cat is much more at home between the warm, cozy sofa cushions of civilization.

The ability to lord over the indomitable, snarling wildcat—to tame the powerful predators and have them submit—has been the desire of mankind for many centuries. The ancient Egyptians surrounded themselves with powerful lions during battles to instill fear in their enemies. The fact that this endeavor was not very successful is another matter. What could be more natural to humans than to create a new breed? A mini-predator, jungle-style, with polka dots or stripes that resemble the big cats—but with a far more cuddly nature.

The dream of living with a wildcat has been realized with the help of three breeds: the ocicat, the Bengal cat, and the Egyptian Mau. While the marbled Bengal has made a triumphal march through Europe, winning many fans, the colorful Egyptian Mau and the ocicat are far less popular. However, ocicats have many admirers in the United States.

A Small Ocelot

So how did it all begin? In 1960s America, Virginia Daly bred a Siamese-Abyssinian-cross with a Siamese cat, and a few weeks later, her dream was fulfilled: snuggled in the box were kittens not only with ticked masks, but also kittens with spotted fur. The random breeding was the beginning of the ocicat evolution.

It was, perhaps, an advantage that the first breeding standards for these little predators did not appear until 1986. Over twenty years, breeders had a chance to iron out any problems with the breed, and in 1987, TICA and ACFA bestowed the breed with an official recognition and catapulted the spotted beauty into popularity in America.

The Ocicat in Europe

In Europe, there was only muted applause as the curtains opened on the miniature ocelot from the United States. Perhaps this low popularity can be attributed to the fact that FIFe had already recognized the Egyptian Mau breed in 1992, as well as the ocicat. It is possible that these new wildcat breeds were too much for rainy Northern Europe because they already had the Bengal. The Bengal had already crept into the hearts of many European breeders, and no other breed could come close. Nonetheless, the fan base of the ocicat breed grew very slowly but steadily. It was found that matings with Abyssinians were beneficial as it gave the breed more substance. Incidentally, experienced ocicat breeders generally agree on the need for targeted outcross breeding programs.

German and English breeders received a lot of praise for the color enhancements made to the breed. The cinnamon color (also known as sorrel) is thanks to them, and they were also one step ahead with the enriching of the attractive detail of the ocicat fur—something that no fan of the spotted cat would want to miss out on. American breeders promptly took this breed under their wing and imported these cinnamon beauties to the United States.

Russian Blue

Build: medium, elegant

Head: short, wedge shaped

Eyes: green, lively, wide set, large, almond shaped

Body: elongated; medium-strength bone structure

Tail: long, tapering

Coat: short, dense, very fine, silky, soft, plushy, double coated

Color: pure, uniform blue with a silver sheen; medium blue is preferred

Pure elegance in a metallic, shimmering coat

The big green eyes light up like emeralds. A silvery blue, lustrous fur coat and the muscular, medium-build body creates the impression of a cat made of precious metal, with brilliant, mysterious eyes. It is with good reason that the Russian blue is described by many admirers as the aristocrat of the cat world. Their grace and unique kind of elegance is fascinating to watch, as they stalk on silent paws. The fascination continues to build as you run your fingers gently over the shimmering blue fur coat.

Is this really cat's fur, or is it a piece of plush velvet fabric you are touching? The short, silky hair is subtle and surprises you with the density of its double coat. The warm undercoat and attractive outercoat are of exactly the same length, resulting in an unusually plush texture. Fans of this stunningly beautiful cat are convinced that the fur is incomparable with any other breed.

Mysterious

It is rumored that this purring kitty cat is extremely mysterious and difficult to comprehend. Russian blues have apparently made it their life's work to maintain this reputation; when they fix their green eyes on you and the tips of their shimmering silver coat shine in the sun, one really gets the idea they are standing before a mysterious being.

You feel a roller coaster of emotions. On the one hand, this cat has a beguiling elegance and beauty, with an almost irresistible appeal. On the other hand, she displays a cold, distinguished aloofness. The blue beauties are far above jumping to their owners' every whim. They show a healthy detachment toward strangers, and new people will undergo a precise, lengthy inspection before they are permitted to touch this cat.

Even Their Origin Is a Mystery

So to whom do we owe the existence of this breathtaking beauty? When did this aristocratic cat first appear? There are numerous theories as to the origin of this breed but nothing concrete about this extraordinary cat's past. Supposedly, it is one of the oldest short-haired breeds of all. The earliest verifiable information is rather shocking: apparently the sleek blue cats were misused for their fur. Contemporary literature tells of cuffs and collars on dress coats, embellished with the fur of the Russian blue.

It is understood that the first Russian blue was presented in England in 1880 and caused quite a stir with its wedge-shaped face, thick whiskers, and silvery, plushy fur. Velvety fur with such a shimmering reflection had never been seen before in rainy old England.

During World War II, the burgeoning breed almost came to a standstill. By the mid-1940s, the breed was virtually extinct. In England, breeders resorted to using blue Siamese, which not only helped to preserve the Russian blue breed but also gave it quite a makeover as well. In the mid-1960s, attempts were made to return to the older Russian blue breed style and this soon made an appearance on the international breeding scene.

Limited, careful breeding of the Russian blue has ensured a pedigree with a strict standard; this breed must be short-haired and may have no white markings. Medallions or white patches on the belly are undesirable, as are long-haired or semilonghair ancestors in the pedigree. The ultimate goal is to preserve the unique appearance and purity of the breed.

Snowshoe

Build: medium, elegant

Head: broad, modified wedge shape with rounded contours

Eyes: walnut shaped, longer than they are wide, blue

Body: medium size, medium-sized bone structure and medium-sized musculature

Tail: medium to long

Coat: short to medium length; no noticeable undercoat; fine, shiny, lies flat against body

Color: seal, blue, chocolate, lilac, red, cream, cinnamon, fawn, or white solid points; tabby point, tortoiseshell points, tortoiseshell tabby points; clearly defined markings that match body color; all four paws must be white; white coloring is allowed on the body; preferred pattern is an upside-down V on the face with white paws

Meet the cat with white snow boots.

Large, deep blue eyes with a unique sparkling expression and white paws are without question the most prominent characteristics of the snowshoe cat. The origin of the imaginative name of this highly intelligent cat is obvious: the striking white paws give the appearance of a cat that has run through fresh powder snow. The result of a cross between a Siamese cat and a bicolor American shorthair, this breed is still relatively young. The first snowshoe kitten was born toward the end of the 1960s. This spectacular achievement was thanks to the ambition of an American cat lover and breeder from Philadelphia.

In 1974, the American Cat Association (ACA) and the Cat Fanciers' Association (CFA) recognized the snowshoe breed as an experimental breed. Although the official recognition encouraged some interest, the breed stagnated for a while. Despite this, enthusiastic supporters of the snowshoe cat remained active. In September 1982, they sought championship status from the Cat Fanciers Federation (CFF), and a year later, the first snowshoe cat received a champion title. Meanwhile, this breed also received champion status from the American Cat Fanciers Association (ACFA), the International Cat Association (TICA), and the World Cat Federation (WCF), among others.

Overall Impression

The snowshoe cat has an extraordinary appearance: the medium-size cat is a combination of Siamese markings and the muscular body of a bicolor American shorthair with four white paws thrown into the mix. In addition, the robustness of its short-haired ancestors, and the elongated body influenced by Oriental blood all combine to give this snowshoe cat its unusual appearance. This breed is very well proportioned; it is neither too large nor too small. The solid, muscular body gives the snowshoe cat its power and agility. The TICA standard compares this breed's appearance with that of a track athlete; a weight-lifter-type of build is undesirable.

The unique combination of dark colorpoints, white coat color, and a short coat of fur makes for a striking appearance. The snowshoe cat's extraordinary beauty reaches its full potential when the contrast between body color and colorpoints is sharp and symmetrical.

Snowshoe cats are smart little creatures. They communicate happily with their humans and have been compared to Siamese but slightly less talkative. Their voices are often described as melodic and soft. Fans of the breed have praised the adaptability of the confident four-legged beauty. Other pets (cats and dogs) are usually very well tolerated. Snowshoe cats are available in seal point, blue point, chocolate point, lilac point, cinnamon, and fawn. Seal point and blue point are the traditional snowshoe colors. The coat is short to medium length, soft, close fitting, and has a slightly coarse texture with a silky sheen. The undercoat is virtually nonexistent.

Personality

Snowshoe cats are intelligent and personable. Their friendly nature makes it easy for them to fit into a household with other pets, and their adaptability makes them relatively uncomplicated family members. The cross with American shorthair certainly contributed to the robust and balanced character of the snowshoe cat. He is

playful, lively, and extremely self-aware. Lovers of this breed rave about its gentle, tender personality.

Sokoke

Build: sleek African wildcat

Head: small in relation to body; a modified wedge shape; flat skull

Eyes: large, wide set, slightly almond shaped and slanted

Body: medium length, slender, well muscled; strong bone structure

Tail: medium length, broader at base than at tip

Coat: very short, close fitting, shiny, not silky; very slight or no undercoat

Color: all shades of black tabby; same for blotched tabbies

Meet the wildcat from the African rain forest.

The Arabuko-Sokoke rain forest in Kenya is home to the very rare Sokoke cat. This area is considered one of the last rain forest areas in East Africa. The species-rich forest is home to not just cats, but is also the home of the Giriama tribe. The locals have been acquainted with these cats for a long time. This breed did not have a wide audience until the late 1970s when farmer Jeni Slater discovered a litter of kittens on her land with no mother.

She took in the little orphans and gave them love and affection. She marveled at the astonishing familiarity of these wildcats. A Danish cat enthusiast took some examples of this breed to Europe and observed how readily these cats took to life in northern Europe. This exotic breed was officially recognized at the beginning of the 1990s. Most specimens are found in Denmark, Norway, and Finland. There are also small numbers living in the United States, Italy, and Germany.

A Pack of Hunters

Most active breeders are found in Denmark, although there are only a small number of breeders there. Heide and Ole Lund Sørensen and Anita Engebakken are the most experienced of the Sokoke breeders and have made some interesting observations over the years: "After our group of Sokokes were put in a fenced yard with an area of approximately [6,458 square feet], we were able to observe the cats, especially at dusk. They are pack animals without a doubt, which not only like to sleep huddled together, but they also hunt together, too. Whether it is hunting for birds or just play hunting with each other, again we were able to make the same fascinating observation: Sokokes encircle their victims, giving each other signals, meaning that they actually communicate with each other during the hunt," report the Sørensens. How they behave when they capture their prey is reminiscent of the big cats. The Sokokes beat their prey with their hind legs, which is a hunting technique of African savanna lions when they catch antelope.

Sixth Sense

It is not only their ingenious hunting technique that took the Danes by surprise: "These cats have a very strong sixth sense. It is almost impossible to give Sokoke cats medical treatment. When one cat has been treated with eye drops or worming medicine, she returns to the group and warns them all using a special language unknown to us. The whole pack immediately flees and nothing can tempt them back near us for the rest of the day."

There are other unusual characteristics: mothers give birth to their Sokoke kittens standing up and the little ones are almost independent from birth. "As a rule, after four or five days, the kittens have not even opened their eyes when they begin to explore their environment on wobbly legs," report Heidi and Ole Lund Sørensen.

Such behavior suggests that Sokoke cats can only survive in the wild if the little ones are independent as soon as possible. Interestingly, these kittens do not shy away from contact with humans as you would expect from a wildcat

breed. "Once a person approaches, the kittens jump up and follow the sound of the voice to make contact," says the breeder.

Special Requirements

Nevertheless, Sokoke cats are not your typical domestic cats. They have very special requirements and make high demands on their owners. So that this regal cat can live it up in style, she should be provided with a generous enclosure. This cat also requires African temperatures. The Sørensen family keeps the temperature of the cattery at a comfortable 73°F and all beds are equipped with additional heat sources. So there are many things to take into account before a prospective owner can take these little wildcats home.

Somali

Build: medium

Head: wedge-shaped head; broad forehead; soft contours

Eyes: large, almond shaped; amber, green, or yellow; outlined by the same color as ticking

Body: solid, smooth, muscular

Tail: long, tapering, broad at base, very fluffy

Coat: fine, very dense, medium length, shorter on shoulders

Color: same as Abyssinian: two or three color bands on each hair with dark tips; ruddy (reddish brown), blue, sorrel (red), beige-fawn, and silver varieties

The Somali is an Abyssinian in a semilonghair coat.

It seems hard to believe that Somali cats were originally reported to be a product of pure chance. The beautiful, amazingly intelligent, tireless, open-minded cats, now bred in all colors of the Abyssinian breed, have a captivating appeal. Somalis have a worldwide popularity and also many passionate, knowledgeable breeders.

The story begins in Somalia in the 1950s and moves on to the United States, Canada, New Zealand, and Australia. Apparently, there were, at this time, many long-haired Abyssinian kittens, which were very desirable to breeders. If you were to examine the pedigree papers of the early Abyssinian generations, you would see that many animals were registered as being of unknown origin, "half-Abyssinian," or "African wildcat." Siamese cats were also involved in the development of this breed. The crossing of different breeds meant that in many litters of kittens there was the odd long-haired kitten, now known as a Somali. The Somali, however, is no longer known as a long-haired Abyssinian; it is now an independent breed with a specific look and character. Although it is still permitted to use Abyssinians to increase the gene pool of Somali cats, this does not apply vice versa.

The Road to Recognition

If it had not been for the pioneering spirit of the breeders who recognized the beauty of the Somali, this semilonghair version of the Abyssinian might not exist today. A small group of breeders and cat fans accompanied these long-haired beauties on the road to recognition, ensuring that they were finally officially recognized as a breed.

May 1, 1979, is a milestone for the Somali breed. On this day, the largest American cat association, the Cat Fanciers' Association (CFA), awarded the breed with championship status, officially recognizing the ruddy and sorrel colors. Breed standards were also established. A year earlier, breeders proudly presented the committee of judges with one hundred twenty-five Somalis in order gain recognition of the breed. The year 1979 also saw the founding of the Somali Cat Society.

At that time, the name Somali (after the African country of Somalia) was inspired by the naming of the Abyssinian breed after the African country Abyssinia (now Ethiopia), even though neither breed has anything to do with the continent of Africa.

Three years after the recognition by the CFA came recognition by the FIFe in Germany, and the colors blue and fawn were included. It took just a year for the silver color varieties to be recognized.

Wild Colors

Although Somali cats are admired for their remarkable variety of colors, the wild colors are the most represented color variety. The reddish brown tone of this very attractive color is reminiscent of fired clay. The ticking of the coat should be black. Experts put great emphasis on the contrast of the banded fur: sorrel

Somalis should have chocolate-colored ticking; blue gray cats should have dark blue ticking; and fawn-colored cats should have a cocoa brown ticking. Each fur type has a full set of Somali stripes; this also applies to silver varieties of the breed.

Sphynx

Build: muscular

Head: slightly longer than it is wide

Eyes: lemon shaped, large, slanted

Body: medium length, hard, muscular, not dainty

Tail: slender, wider at the base

Coat: skin appears hairless; sometimes has a short, soft down; wrinkles around the nose, between the ears, and around the shoulders; skin feels like suede

Color: all color varieties, any amount of white is allowed

This cat is naked and unusually striking.

When it comes to sphynx cats, there are no compromises; people either find them fascinating or just plain ugly. What many ignorant people equate with being sick, disgusting, or abnormal can be, in reality, perfectly healthy, cheerful, and very affectionate. Just because a cat does not have fur, it does not mean it is more susceptible to disease or has a shorter life expectancy. Fans of this unusual breed love the delicate, warm skin of these cats and become very animated when discussing their loving and affectionate natures. There must have always been hairless cat fans—as well as hairless dog fans—because the Aztecs reportedly bred these cats. In 1830, the German biologist Johann Rudolph Renger described hairless cats in his book *Natural History of Paraguayan Mammals*. The next clue is a black-and-white photo from 1902 that shows two "Mexican hairless" cats. In the photo, one can see the bodies of these cats have at least two different color pigmentations. Their legs and faces are a brighter color than the rest of them.

J. Shinick, from Albuquerque, New Mexico, wrote an article at the beginning of the twentieth century, where he made some interesting references as to the history of these cats: "These cats were acquired from some Indians a few miles away. The old Jesuit Father believes these are the last of the Aztec breed, and they are known only in New Mexico."

Shinick acquired two of these cats named Nellie and Dick. After the sudden death of the male cat, he attempted to find another hairless male cat but was unsuccessful. It seemed to the breeder that this breed would eventually become extinct.

Since that time, there has been sporadic evidence of hairless cats. It could be said that these cats are a freak of nature, but some people grew fond of them all the same. Today, there is a small but incredibly enthusiastic number of people who rave about these unusual creatures.

Recessive Gene

The lack of fur is caused by a recessive gene that can be carried over many generations without any impact on the cats' appearance. It is not until two cats with this recessive gene are mated together that naked kittens will be produced. Consequently, cats with normal fur play a role in the sphynx breed. For example, the fluffy cat Jezebel in the United States is considered a milestone of the modern breed. The European lineage was said to have begun from the cats Punkie and Paloma. Supposedly, these two cats were discovered by inexperienced cat lovers at the end of the 1970s. They lived an existence as stray cats. At first, it was believed they had a contagious disease, but as it turned out, these cats were actually sphynxes. They were exported to Holland, where the breeder Hugo Hernandez was absolutely delighted with them. He already had a sphynx cat and was thrilled to have "fresh genes" in order to be able to continue the breed. To establish breeding, it was necessary

to interbreed with Devon rex cats to avoid health problems caused by a too-small gene pool.

Skin Like Suede

Considering their average body size, sphynx cats are surprisingly strong. They have firm, muscular bodies, including rounded, but not fat, stomachs. The most notable characteristic is, of course, the skin, which, on closer inspection, is covered with a fine down. When you stroke the skin, you will notice it is soft and warm, like suede. The folds in the skin are rare and according to the standard, highly desirable, particularly around the nose, ears, and shoulders.

Tailless Breeds

Japanese Bobtail

Build: medium size, short tail

Head: an almost perfect isosceles triangle with gently curved lines

Eyes: large, oval, wide eyed, watchful

Body: long, slender, elegant

Tail: about 2–3 inches long, strong, straight or curved, stands upright

Coat: short, soft, silky

Color: all colors other than silver or golden shaded/shell, ticked tabby, and colorpoint

Kurilian Bobtail (shorthair/longhair)

Build: medium to large

Head: large, trapezoidal with rounded contours

Eyes: rounded, slightly slanted

Body: compact, muscular; strong bone structure

Tail: several curves or angles, 1–3 inches long

Coat: short-haired variety: dense, fine texture; stiff whiskers; moderate undercoat; **long-haired variety:** semilonghair; thin undercoat; shirtfront, ruff, breeches

Cats without rudders!

These cat breeds are not actually tailless, but they do not have normal-length tails. There are four different tailless breeds recognized by the Fédération Internationale Féline: the Japanese bobtail, the Kurilian bobtail shorthair, the Kurilian bobtail longhair, and the Manx. The World Cat Federation accepts additional tailless breeds: the Cymric (also known as a long-haired Manx), the Karelian bobtail, and the Mekong bobtail. In the United States, there are even more breeds, for example, the American bobtail. Whether you prefer a cat to have a tail or not is purely a matter of personal taste. Only one thing is sure: this unusual feature is not usually harmful to a cat's health in any way.

Japanese Bobtail

This breed, seen as lucky in Japan, has a small, stubby tail, similar to a pom-pom. The stubby tail resembles a rabbit's tail. The much-coveted variety, the *mi-ke* (literally meaning "triple hair"), also called calico, has many enthusiastic fans. These cats are mostly white with red and black patches. The patches should be contrasted and clearly separate from each other. The short tail is the result of a genetic mutation. It should be two to three inches long, but some tails reach up to five inches in length. Others have several curves or angles in the tail.

In medieval Japan, this cat was seen as a lucky charm and a symbol of hospitality. Historical drawings and sculptures are evidence of their popularity. Even today, there are families in Japan who keep small Japanese bobtail statues with raised paws on their doorsteps to welcome guests.

This breed is said to have a curious and attentive nature. Their openness and interest in the world around them makes them very pleasant family members, and they come in all sorts of color varieties.

Kurilian Bobtail

The Kurilian bobtail can be long-haired or short-haired. The tail is even shorter than that of the Japanese bobtail. It is only one to three inches in length and has curves or angles. It is either stiff or flexible.

Kurilian bobtails are medium- to large-sized cats with strong, compact bodies. One of their characteristics is a slightly arched back that reaches all the way from the shoulders to the hind legs. Short-haired Kurilian bobtails have a thick coat with a finer texture

and well-developed whiskers. The long-haired variety has a significantly longer coat, small whiskers, a full ruff, and a fine undercoat.

Manx

For Manx cats, the differences are not in the coat length but in the stubby tail. The "rumpy" has a gap at the end of the spine and a tuft of hair on the rump where the tail would have been. The "rumpy riser" has a bump of cartilage under the fur but it does not affect the tailless appearance of the cat. The "stumpy" has a very short but noticeable tail that is often irregularly shaped and should not be any longer than about one and a quarter inches. All colors and patterns are allowed according to the breed standard.

Tailless cats usually do not have any problems with balance or movement.

(Kurilian bobtail cont.)

Color: all colors except colorpoints, chocolate, cinnamon, fawn, lilac, and any of these colors combined with white

Manx

Build: medium size, short body, large flanks

Head: large, round, chubby

Eyes: large, round

Body: strong, compact

Tail: rumpy: gap at the end of the spine; **rumpy riser:** cartilage at end of spine under fur; **stumpy:** a short, often irregularly shaped stump, maximum 1.2 inches long

Coat: short-haired

Colors: all colors

Oriental Breeds

< A Balinese with spectacular blue eyes

> Oriental shorthairs have slim builds.

>> Siamese cats are bred in many beautiful colors.

The Oriental shorthair, Oriental longhair (Javanese), Siamese, and Balinese breeds all belong to the Oriental cat family, known as category IV of the FIFe. The genetic connection is easily explained: the Oriental longhair, which some cat associations call the Mandarin or Javanese, was created by mating a Balinese and an Oriental shorthair. It is, therefore, a long-haired version of the Oriental shorthair. Balinese cats are long-haired versions of Siamese cats. Furthermore, Oriental shorthairs are the solid-colored relatives of the Siamese. Together with the Persians, Oriental shorthairs share the reputation of being the most traditional of all the exotic breeds. Numerous other breeds and color varieties owe their existence to Oriental shorthairs and Persians.

> The Same Character

Cats in the Oriental family are very similar in character; they tend to have good natures but can be arrogant, and they enjoy boisterous games and pranks. A well-furnished apartment offers plenty of opportunities to create mischief. When they are playing, they will run over tables and chairs, and any movable object is fair game.

However, the complex nature of these beautiful creatures with mysterious eyes also includes some very heartwarming characteristics. Orientals can be very quiet, polite, and tender. They like to spend hours on the sofa purring soothingly. Orientals tend to seek out contact with their humans and will follow them everywhere. These cats will also observe everything their owners do!

› Strong Personalities

These slender, graceful cats are said to be incredibly sociable animals. In fact, Oriental cats prefer to live in a large diverse group and they will all get along just fine—very rarely does fur fly between these animals. They also get along with other cat breeds and even dogs—as long as these dogs are cat friendly, of course. Oriental cats feel most at home in a lively, sociable household. However, there is a very special rule for your sociable Oriental. Rule number one: Orientals call the

shots. These slender beauties are quicker thinking than any other four-legged friend, so it is hardly surprising they will appoint themselves as leader of the pack.

› Arrival in England

According to the relevant literature, the first Oriental arrived in England in 1850 and created a furor among cat fanciers. It is alleged that the exotic imports came in two variations: a blue-eyed colorpoint with a delicate pale-colored body, known then as the "royal Siam," and the "foreign," a solid-colored Oriental cat with amber eyes. Some cat experts say that this cat could have been a Burmese.

Due to the beauty of the royal Siam's colorpoints, much praise was heaped on this cat, and the solid-colored foreign lived very much in the shadow of the royal Siam. The foreign walked among Russian blues, Burmese cats, and British shorthairs, so it did not get the recognition it deserved. The year 1902 saw the first breed standard for Oriental cats, and selective breeding of these cats was said to have begun in the 1950s.

› A Mysterious Look

An Oriental shorthair cat has a special way of conquering his owner's heart. His intelligent-looking gaze penetrates deep in the soul of a human, and he will quickly figure out whether someone is a nice, cat-friendly person or someone to be wary of. Within a few seconds, this graceful cat has decided whether or not he likes you, and his first impressions stay with him forever.

Oriental shorthairs are masters of improvisation. They monopolize their humans and decide when and where cuddles should take place. If you try to put your cat down when he has not finished his cuddle, he will protest loudly! All representatives of the Oriental family are very precocious (they mature early) and have loud, expressive voices.

Balinese >78
Oriental Longhair >80
Oriental Shorthair >82
Siamese >84

Balinese

Build: Oriental

Head: medium size, well proportioned, wedge shaped

Eyes: medium size, neither protruding nor deep set, almond shaped, slightly slanted; a pure, clear blue color

Body: long, slender, muscular, graceful, elegant

Tail: very long, thin, tapering

Coat: fine, silky, medium length on the body; slightly longer on the ruff, shoulders, and tail; no woolly undercoat

Color: white, solid point, tabby point; **Points:** masked face and markings on ears, legs, and tail

This cat is admired for its gracefulness.

This beautiful breed has nothing to do with the Indonesian island of Bali, but its name was said to have been inspired by the Balinese culture. The origin of these graceful cats is actually the United States, where the breed was developed in the 1950s. From a Balinese breeder's point of view, these cats are considered to be long-haired Siamese cats. Therefore, Balinese cats have the same breeding standard, apart from the coat requirements. Long-haired Siamese cats have probably always appeared in litters of short-haired kittens, but no one really advertised this fact. These kittens would not have been right for cat shows or further breeding, and it took some time before their unique beauty was appreciated.

"The charm and grace of these cats is similar to the Balinese temple dancers," says Helen Smith, a pioneer of Balinese breeding who helped spread the word about this breed. The experienced Siamese breeder cultivated a taste for the long-haired kitten that from time to time appeared in one of her litters of kittens. She did not see this as a bad thing. In fact, her obvious enthusiasm led to the recognition of a highly attractive variant of the Siamese breed.

The Pioneer of the Breed

Helen Smith soon realized her dreams for this breed. She became involved in a breeding program that led to eight Balinese cats being exhibited at a cat show in the United States. Seven years later, there were twenty-three of these beautiful cats to admire. The Cat Fanciers' Association recognized this new breed in 1970, and, in the same year, the Balinese breed was awarded championship status. After this breed had caused a stir in America, Europe began to take an interest in these semilonghair cats. In 1983, official recognition from the FIFe paved the way for successful breeding and more cat show success.

However, anyone dreaming of a Bali-boom would be sorely disappointed. There were only a handful of dedicated

Balinese breeders, and this has not changed much over the years. Balinese still belong to the rare breeds of cats and by no means enjoy the popularity of other breeds.

Balinese and Company

Balinese cats are outgoing and sociable; they need company and plenty of it. People who are never home should not own one of these cats or at least not just keep one cat on its own. Solitude is not pleasant for this cat, and she can become quite depressed if left to her own devices. The presence of other cats can help prevent this, but Balinese cats are happiest in the company of their beloved humans.

Loud and Precocious

Balinese are among the most precocious cat breeds. Females often go through their first heat cycle at the tender age of just six months, and the tomcat also reaches adolescence very early on. It is at this point when the inexperienced Balinese owner will become acquainted with the vociferous voices of these graceful beauties.

When comparing the appearance of "modern" Balinese cats to those of the first generation, you will notice a significant difference: the entire phenotype has changed. At the same time, a degree of perfection and expressiveness has been found in these cats. Regular crossings with Siamese have helped contribute to the development of the breed, which is now much admired. This remarkable result is the reward for decades of work from a relatively small group of dedicated breeders.

Oriental Longhair (Javanese)

Build: Oriental

Head: medium size, well proportioned, wedge shaped

Eyes: medium size, almond shaped, slightly slanted, deep green color

Body: long, slender, well muscled, graceful, elegant

Tail: very long, thin, tapering

Coat: fine, silky, medium length on the body; slightly longer on the ruff, shoulders, and tail; no woolly undercoat

Color: solid color, tortoiseshell, smoke, tabby, silver tabby, van/harlequin/bicolor, van/harlequin/bicolor smoke, van/harlequin/bicolor tabby, van/harlequin/bicolor silver tabby

Meet the little diva with a pretty fur coat.

As you may have read in the previous section, Balinese cats do not hail from Bali in Indonesia. Similarly, Javanese cats do not come from Java; the romantic name is nothing but an Indonesian-inspired idea thought up by the British. As previously mentioned, the Javanese breed originated from crossing a Balinese with an Oriental shorthair cat.

Eye-Catching Coat

Not only do Javanese cats have expressive green eyes, but they enchant cat lovers with their fine, silky coat. The fur is medium length on the body; on the ruff, shoulders, and the tail, the fur is ideally plumed and slightly longer. Like the Balinese breed, Javanese do not have woolly undercoats.

Those who are not fans of grooming, however, can breathe a sigh of relief; Javanese are extremely easy to care for. Occasional brushing and combing is enough and ideal to ensure they maintain a well-groomed appearance. Furthermore, a clean environment, healthy food, and exercise will not only benefit the cat's well-being but also enhance the appearance of his coat.

Oriental Shorthairs in a Long-Haired Coat

From a purely visual point of view, Javanese are Oriental shorthairs with semilonghair fur. Consequently, they have the same standard as the Oriental shorthairs, apart from the requirements for the medium-length coat, of course.

Javanese are medium-sized, slender cats and give the impression of elegance and grace. The lines of his body seem to flow smoothly, and the muscles are visible. The shoulders should not be wider than the hips. The very long, thin tail, which is not wide at the base, has a fine tip to it.

The Characteristic Head

The medium-sized head, one of the breeding challenges, should sit on a long, slender neck, and be in proportion to the body. The head itself should have good proportions. It should be wedge shaped and angular. The clearly visible wedge should begin at the nose and widen on both sides up toward the ears. A so-called break at the whiskers is undesirable. The skull of the Javanese, when seen in profile, should be slightly convex. The line of the long, straight nose should not have any dents in it, the nose should be narrow, and the chin should be slightly rounded. There should be an imaginary vertical line running from the tip of the chin to the tip of the nose.

The large, pointed ears of the Javanese are conspicuous and eye catching. They are wide at the base and add to the width of the wedge-shaped head. The eyes should be of medium size and not be too prominent nor too deep set. They should be almond shaped and at a slight angle to the nose. This emphasizes the wedge-shaped head. Javanese have wonderful green eyes; ideally, the color should be clear, bright, and intense.

Oriental Shorthair

Build: strikingly elegant with very large ears

Head: medium size, wedge shaped, well proportioned

Eyes: medium size, not too deep set, not prominent, almond shaped, slightly slanted, green

Body: medium size, elongated, lean, muscular, elegant

Tail: long, thin at the base, ends in a whip-like tip

Coat: smooth, fine, glossy, lies flat against body

Color: solid color, tortoiseshell, smoke, tabby, silver tabby, van/harlequin/bicolor, van/harlequin/bicolor smoke, van/harlequin/bicolor tabby, van/harlequin/bicolor silver tabby

These are lovable charmers with bat-like ears.

Is your home governed by an Oriental shorthair? Then you will certainly be familiar with the unique character and extraordinary appearance of this sleek hunter. So what is so special about him? Well those who are already accustomed to the magnificent size of a fluffy Norwegian forest cat will look twice when surrounded by the slender silhouette of this quietly creeping cat and see the traditional grace of a feline friend in all his glory.

If you have not had the pleasure of meeting one of these Oriental beauties, it is highly recommended you take a look. It is a very special experience to see the merging of the wonderful lightness of movement and noble elegance. Oriental shorthairs are occasionally seen at cat shows; however, there are not many of them representing the breed.

These intelligent go-getters are not mass-produced, rather they belong to one of the rare breeds, worshipped by a small circle of cat lovers.

Very Confident

Similar to Siamese cats, they have enormous self-confidence. Most Oriental shorthairs do not suffer from an inferiority complex or any similar inhibitions. Anyone who approaches them—depending on the individual character of the cat—is treated with resolute kindness, playful attacks, or domineering territorial behavior. If someone is clearly not a cat lover, the Oriental shorthair will return the contempt.

Thanks to the chemistry that usually exists between cat and human, it does not take long to break the ice.

Before you know it, a wedge-shaped head is pressing against your hand, demanding to be petted with a loud, rolling purr.

Plain Beautiful

Oriental shorthair cats are the solid-colored relatives of the Siamese cats. In the Middle Ages and the Renaissance, Oriental cats supposedly lived predominantly in Thailand and were not known to European cat lovers. A traveler may have caught a glimpse one of these graceful cats' ancestors, but there is nothing concrete to prove this is so. From Thai writings, it is known that this slender beauty was temporarily given the high status of being Thailand's national cat and was highly thought of in aristocratic circles.

Tremendously Vocal Personalities

Oriental shorthairs are not afraid to express themselves and are sometimes reported to be very needy. Like most other Oriental cat breeds, even as kittens they have very powerful voices, and feel the need to communicate loudly with one another within the litter. So if you want to share your home with an Oriental shorthair, you will need to get used to the talkative ways of your four-legged friend. He will follow you everywhere and certainly has plenty to say. This need for constant vocal expression is quite endearing but can become your worst nightmare if your female cat is in heat. She can yowl for days on end, much to the distress of her

long-suffering owners. It is a good idea to have her spayed, or else ensure that your walls are well insulated and you have a pair of earplugs at hand.

Siamese

Build: elegant

Head: medium size, wedge shaped, well proportioned

Eyes: medium size, almond shaped, slightly slanted, deep blue

Body: medium size, long, lean, muscular, elegant

Tail: long, whip-like, thin at tip

Coat: short, fine, glossy, smooth, lies flat against body

Color: seal point, chocolate point, blue point, lilac point, red point, cream point, tabby point, tortoiseshell point

This cat has a big personality.

There are many tall tales and legends surrounding the history of the Siamese cat, including various embellished stories that attempt to explain the kink in the tail, characteristic of the early imported Siamese. It is said that a Thai princess took off her precious rings before bathing and kept them on her Siamese cat's tail. A kink in the tail ensured that the precious jewels did not fall off.

Another legend tells how a pair of Siamese cats guarded the gold cup of the Buddha. When all the men of Siam fled their homes to protect their homeland, there was no one to guard the gold cup of the Buddha. In the temple were Tien and Chula, a pair of Siamese cats. Tien left Chula to protect the treasure and go in search of a priest. As time passed, the long hours turned into days and weeks, and Chula kept her eyes on the sacred cup, curling her tail around it so it could not be stolen. The cat was so committed to her task, she stayed in the temple to give birth to her kittens. Not for one moment did she turn away from the cup, and she gave birth to kittens that were just like herself, with slanted eyes and kinked tails. The kittens had blue eyes, the color of the sky; this was the Buddha's reward for their loyalty.

Power and Vitality

Almond-shaped eyes and kinked tails are a result of years of successful breeding. Breeders managed to create a flawless beauty with a magical spirit that so many cat lovers appreciate.

It is said that you can never feel alone when you are with a Siamese cat. These cats have an unusual appreciation for their people and will follow them from room to room to stay close by their sides.

Their sociability is pronounced by their readiness to communicate. They keep up a constant, merry chatter in a very loud voice. A female Siamese cat in heat can really test the nerves of her owner! Climbing and jumping are important requirements for a Siamese cat. Full of grace and vivacity, these athletic gymnasts will clamber over anything in the house.

Controversial Beauty

The unique appearance of the Siamese cat has always been a topic of debate. Some feel it is the most beautiful cat in the world, while others find this slender

cat, with his triangular head and strikingly large ears, highly unattractive. Since their first appearance in Europe in about 1871, these elegant masked cats have caused a stir and caused opinion to be divided. Some referred to this animal as "the nightmare cat with a marten's face," while others boasted about the "elegant beauty from Thailand." Not much has changed over the years.

Thai Roots

In the Thai National Library in Bangkok, there is a book that contains what is considered to be one of the earliest writings about the Siamese cat. This book is considered to be the world's oldest book on the subject of cats and is priceless. It was written between 1350 and 1767, in Ayudha, the old capital of Siam, now Thailand. In one chapter of the book, there is a description of a brightly colored cat with dark markings on his tail, paws, and ears. Is this the first ever description of a Siamese cat, or is it just coincidence that this cat, once called the Vichien Mas, is also described as being extremely vocal?

It is believed that Siamese cats originated from Thailand a very long time ago. These cats were worshipped, and they were especially popular with nobility. The phrase "noble moon diamonds" appeared in many old documents and leaves no doubt that Siamese cats were considered to be very special indeed. It seems that the breed was very rare in Thailand and would only have been encountered in the homes of very wealthy families.

Breeds Recognized by the World

◁ **The Highland fold (left) and the Highland straight are extremely rare breeds.**

While the time-honored governing body of FIFe is slightly more conservative about its recognition of new cat breeds, the World Cat Federation (WCF) has proved to be slightly more adventurous. This federation, based in Germany, recognizes many wonderful breeds that are becoming increasingly popular.

‣ Folded Ears and Long-Haired British

We will begin with the Highland fold and Scottish fold whose breeding has been extremely challenging and requires considerable expertise. Not all cat lovers are fans of these breeds, but they certainly have quite a following, nevertheless. While the Highland fold belongs in the semilonghair category of the WCF, the Scottish fold belongs in the shorthair group.

The British longhair is one of the five breeds placed in the longhair category. These are referred to as long-haired British shorthairs by some cat organizations, which can seem quite confusing! The long coat is a result of a crossing with Persians and requires daily grooming and regular washing.

‣ Short-Haired Stars

So what does the WCF shorthair group have to offer? The short answer is a lot. For example, there is the merry little Anatoli, which was officially recognized only recently. Since then, these cats have found many fans in countries such as Turkey and Germany.

Less well known, however, are the all-black, orange-eyed Bombay cats that are recognized by the WCF. This "mini-panther" is almost nonexistent in

Cat Federation

Europe. There are still some breeders in the United States, but whether this is sufficient to keep the breed going is uncertain.

Another extremely rare breed is the Kanaani cat, which originates from Israel. This breed was recognized by the WCF in 2000, but it has been through a lot of ups and downs. However, this cat has shown that it is possible to breed a wildcat with a strong domestic streak. Kanaanis are extremely intelligent and always on the go.

Perhaps you are not too fond of wildcats and would prefer a cuddly teddy bear type of cat instead? Then the Selkirk rex could be the one for you. The WCF has added to the rex group (German rex, Cornish rex, Devon rex) with this semilonghair or short-haired cat. Up until recently, Persian, exotic shorthair, and British shorthair genes have contributed to the success of this relatively new breed, but soon this crossbreeding will come to an end, and this breed will have to stand on its own four legs.

＞ Siamese and Oriental Shorthair Group

The Mekong bobtail, Oriental shorthair, Peterbald cats, Siamese, Tonkinese, and Thai cats are listed under the Siamese and Oriental shorthair category of the WCF. Oriental shorthairs and Siamese are also recognized by FIFe; therefore, their profiles can be found in the previous section (see pages 82 and 84). Mekong bobtail, Peterbald cats, and Tonkinese cats are extremely rare. Thai cats are not only very beautiful but also veryy affectionate and sociable. Therefore, it is not surprising that they are becoming increasingly popular.

Anatoli ＞92

Asian ＞104

Australian Mist ＞104

Bombay ＞94

Brazilian Shorthair ＞104

British Longhair ＞90

Celtic Shorthair ＞105

Ceylon ＞102

Don Sphynx ＞104

Kanaani ＞96

Peterbald ＞105

Scottish Fold, Highland Fold ＞88

Selkirk Rex ＞98

Singapura ＞105

Thai ＞100

Tonkinese ＞105

York ＞104

❮ Scottish folds can create the wrong impression when among other cats due to their folded ears. This can lead to misunderstandings in communication.

Scottish and Highland Fold

Build: balanced, good proportions

Head: rounded; rounded cheeks and well-rounded whiskers

Eyes: wide, large, round; friendly expression

Body: medium size, rounded, even; moderate-sized bone structure

Tail: medium to long

Coat: Scottish fold: dense, plush, short; **Highland fold:** medium long, soft, crisp texture, long ruff and "trousers"

Colors: all colors and patterns with any amount of white, Siamese points without white

Fans of folded ears will love these breeds.

Whether a cat with folded ears is especially cute or overly fanciful is all down to a question of taste. Those who own these lovable four-legged friends with owl-like faces are quite used to this debate. Ever since these breeds became known, they have divided cat fans into two camps: those who appreciate their extraordinary appearance, and others who find the sight of folded ears very strange and suspect that there lurks a dangerous genetic defect behind these unusual features.

There is no question that the fold is a mutation, but it does not give a cat with folded ears a health disadvantage. Some mutations cause health problems that affect the life expectancy and well-being of an animal, and others simply give an animal a quirky appearance, without any negative impact on health.

Mutations obviously play an important role in the world of cat breeding. A mutation can either be welcomed or unwanted, depending on how it manifests itself. The mating of two carriers with a genetic mutation can often be fraught with problems. Consequently, with respect to breeding, a good knowledge of genetics and a sense of responsibility are essential requirements. Scottish and Highland folds are therefore certainly not a breed for experimental beginners and genetic adventurers.

A Breed With Good Proportions

Scottish folds, which were bred from Scottish farm cats, are a very symmetrical breed. This cat's well-rounded head merges into a short neck with a strong chin, a well-formed jaw, and rounded cheeks. The cheeks are particularly pronounced in males. The nose is adorned with thick whiskers.

The large, round, wide-open, beautiful eyes are very expressive and are separated by a wide nose. The eye color should harmonize with the coat color. The short nose has a slight curve.

The ears—the real eye-catchers of this breed—are folded forward and downward. Smaller, very tightly folded ears are preferred (some cats have large, loosely folded ears). The ears sit like a cap on the head and outline the rounded skull.

The medium-sized body with its moderate-strength bones is rounded from the shoulder to the pelvis. Short, stumpy or solidly built legs that could restrict mobility are not desirable for this breed. The tapered tail of the Scottish fold should be medium to long and in good proportion to the body. The mobility of this cat is an important criterion.

The ideal coat is dense, plush, medium length, and soft with a crisp texture. It should not be snug but standing away from the body. The fur texture varies according to color and is also influenced by the seasons. The colors of the Scottish fold correspond to those of the Persian, and the cat should have a matching eye color. Other colors and patterns are also permitted; Siamese markings, chocolate, and lavender combinations are also recognized.

Highland Fold

The Highland fold is the semilonghair variant of the Scottish fold. The texture of the medium-length coat is soft and crisp and stands up away from the body. Particularly desirable specimens have a beautiful long ruff and "trousers." Until

1987, Highland folds were known in Germany as Bambinas, which resulted from mating two short-haired cats. This was followed by matings with British shorthairs carrying the longhair gene and Persians.

There are also varieties of the Scottish and Highland folds that have normal ears.

British Longhair

Build: stocky

Head: round, solid, broad skull

Eyes: large, round, wide set, wide eyed

Body: muscular, broad chest and shoulders; powerful, strong back

Tail: short and thick; slightly rounded tip

Coat: long, smooth, dense, stands away from the body; a ruff and "trousers" is preferable; thick, protective coat; coarse, crisp texture for blue coats; texture can vary in all other colors

The blue British longhair has a beautiful coat the color of mist.

Long-haired British breeds have been given many fanciful names that inspire the imagination and keep cat fans guessing: Lowlander, Highlander, and Britannica are among the most popular variants of name for the British longhair, depending on which association or breeder you speak to.

So whether you are rushing out to acquire a Lowlander, Highlander, or a Britannica, this cat really is the dearest, fluffiest creature. Her saucer-shaped eyes give her an inquisitive expression and after much extensive sniffing, she is ready to cuddle and play. Although this charming creature with inviting fur has become increasingly popular, these long-haired British cats are not recognized by every cat association. Along with WCF, TICA has officially recognized this breed while other cat organizations have yet to do so.

Equipped with voluminous, luxurious fur, it is easy to see that the Persian has made an active contribution to this breed. English breeders were happy to note that Persian genes significantly improved the fur quality and also helped weed out some of the other more undesirable long-haired genes that would otherwise have led to a dramatic deterioration of the breed. Thus, the origin of these long-haired beauties is a result of crossing British shorthair breeds with the Persian, which not only gave it the correct fur type but also brought with it a variety of interesting colors. When two British shorthairs are bred, sometimes this Persian long-haired gene will manifest itself. What some breeders regard as undesirable is a welcome delight to others.

Nature

The character of these long-haired cats combines the pride and temperament of British shorthair breeds with the cuddly coziness of a Persian. Like a Persian, the coat of a British longhair requires daily combing to avoid tangles. Regular baths are also recommended.

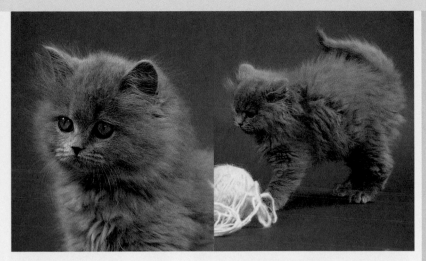

Colors: solid white, black, blue, chocolate, lilac, cinamon, fawn, red, and cream; tortoiseshell varieties of blue, chocolate, lilac, cinnamon, and fawn; all colors mentioned above together with white as bicolor or tricolor; colorpoint in all of these colors (except white); silver or golden tabby, shaded, and shell with or without white; smoke, smoke and white, tabby, tabby and white

There is also no difference between the Persian and the British longhair with regard to the need for affection. A day where she does not get any cuddles is a bad day for this cat! She enjoys close physical contact, having her head rubbed, and her fur stroked by her owner. She is also quite happy to receive affection from other animals, and an exceptionally good-natured dog will make a good companion for this cat. She also loves to curl up to her own kind as well.

Care

Gentle stroking and daily combing is enjoyable for most British longhairs. But not all of these cats are happy to be lap cats; do not force this on her because it could affect her relationship with you. The majority of this breed would prefer to be in close proximity of their people and sit on a cozy couch for hours on end being stroked. Particularly needy cats from this breed will follow their owners' every step and will look

on curiously while they perform even the dullest of daily tasks. Once this has become boring, this cuddly cat will once again retreat to the sofa and emit an incredibly soothing purr, characteristic of this breed.

Anatoli

Build: medium

Head: broad at base, rounded wedge shape

Eyes: relatively large, outer corner of eye slants upwards, slightly almond shaped; green, light yellow to dark amber, or matches coat color; in white cats, also blue or different-colored eyes (one yellow and one blue eye or one green and one blue eye)

Body: strong, muscular; tall, strong legs

Tail: long, slightly curved at tip, strong; dense fur on tail

Coat: short, dense, silky, soft, smooth, lies flat against body, no undercoat

Colors: all colors except lilac, chocolate, cinnamon, fawn, and colorpoints

This is a relatively new breed from Turkey.

In the past few years, Turkish breeds have become increasingly popular. Almost every cat fan has heard of the water-loving Turkish Van and the enchanting, fluffy Turkish Angora. But when it comes to the Anatoli, many people will shrug helplessly and say they have never heard of such a breed. This could be because the breed is relatively new; it was officially recognized in 2000, but it is not represented by all cat associations. It is actually quite difficult to find much information at all on this breed from Lake Van in Turkey. Nevertheless, the Anatoli, also known as the Anatolian or Turkish shorthair, has a lot to offer.

Fans of the breed will tell you that this cat, despite its similarity to the Turkish Van, is a completely independent breed. There has been no demonstrable crossing with other breeds—as far as the small number of breeders are aware. For most Turkish people, the Anatoli is not seen as a pedigree cat; he is known as an excellent rodent catcher that lives on the streets and can be found in the remotest of villages. Nevertheless, these Turkish village cats all have phenotypic similarities. Consequently, it was inevitable that these characteristics would be documented and outlined in a breed standard; however, it was a long time before this breed was officially recognized.

Green Light for the Anatoli

After years of going back and forth, this breed was finally given the recognition it deserved. At a general assembly meeting of the WCF, eighteen out of nineteen board members, each representing a different country, voted with a resounding "yes" to the question of whether the Anatoli should be recognized as an independent breed. Only the Italian representative of the board abstained from voting, which had no effect on the recognition of this breed in the end.

The breeding standard of the Anatoli was almost the same as the Turkish Van with some adjustments. It was also decided that these two breeds could be mated together where necessary. The offspring from these matings are described as a "variant." The new entry in the pedigree family tree was labeled under the heading "breed." That was a big step forward. This paved the way for a promising development for the breeders and friends of the little-known Turkish breed. Nevertheless, the breed today still faces a huge problem: there are far too few dedicated breeders.

The Turks campaigned for their unofficial national cat. They organized exhibitions in the city of Van, where the best examples of this cat could be compared and admired. Van University established a breeding program and the intense scientific interest paid tribute to the Anatolian beauty. Cats from the Van region can today be admired in the Van city zoo in Turkey.

Struggling for Recognition

In Turkey, there was considerable interest in the breed, but what about the rest of the world? These cats are exported to Europe and the United States, and in many cases mistakenly registered as Turkish Vans or Turkish Angoras.

However, breeders in Germany and the Netherlands are working to preserve the breed. The International Turkish Angora and Van Club (ITAVC) of Germany proved after a year-long study that not only did the Anatoli come in a brilliant white but also in many other attractive colors. For this association, there was no question that this breed deserved independent recognition. The breed could be admired at ITAVC cat shows long before the WFC official recognition. The exhibited animals showed a great consistency and received rave reviews.

Playing and Cuddling

Anatolis are lovable and affectionate. This cat has a strong need to play. Owners need to take a little time each day to meet this need, or they could find their cats hanging off their legs or attempting to wear off excess energy during the night. It is a good idea to own more than one of these cats so they can play and cuddle together. These furry whirlwinds have very spirited natures. Do you value your peace and quiet? Then you would be better off opting for a calmer breed than the Anatoli. These excitable cats from Lake Van live their lives at a hundred miles per hour and enjoy every second.

Bombay

Build: medium

Head: attractively rounded; full face with very wide-set eyes; smooth transition into a broad, moderately rounded, well-developed nose; moderate, highly visible stop (where the nose meets the face)

Eyes: round, wide set

Body: medium size, muscular, neither compact nor long

Tail: medium length, straight

Coat: silky texture; fine, dense, shiny

Color: in adult cats, the coat should be black right up to the root; nose and undersides of paws should be black

Meet the mini-panther with the copper-colored eyes!

Things are not looking good for the Bombay. The total number of these cats worldwide is thought to be under one hundred. Most of these animals are not used for breeding, which makes a bad situation even worse. One really has to apply detective skills to find out anything much at all about the fate of this breed. Litters have become increasingly rare around the globe.

There is said to be many similarities between the nature of the Bombay and the Burmese. This idea is certainly not unreasonable, especially since this American breed originated from a cross between a sable/brown Burmese and a black American shorthair.

Bombays are just as happy in a furnished apartment as they are in an enclosed yard. Fans of this breed appreciate the peaceful and harmonious nature of this cat. However, this self-aware breed does not live happily with a pet dog nor its own kind. Their innate dominance can lead to fights and can cause many problems for their owners.

An Intelligent Little Creature

The Bombay is rumored to have a wise head on her shoulders. She is always seeking contact with her people, asking to be stroked, lightly brushing against you, and likes to indulge in boisterous games. Many learn the most amazing tricks: on command they will jump up on a cabinet, retrieve toys, or leap over the outstretched arms of their owner. This is all just child's play for the Bombay. Interestingly, most of these mini-panthers will learn to walk on a leash quite happily. This is unlike many other cat breeds that fight to get their collars off with all their might. The Bombay seems to readily accept being put on a leash, and these cats rejoice in small walks with their owners. There is another peculiarity that the black Bombays share with their relatives, the Burmese cats: they love the warmth of down comforters or other cozy items and will disappear underneath them at any opportunity.

Talkative

The distinctive voice of the Bombay
may not be for everyone, but it is
by no means as intrusive as the
Siamese. Talkativeness is an important
characteristic of the breed; owners will
need to get used to these cats using their
voices willy-nilly.

A precocious breed, the female
Bombay usually reaches sexual maturity
at the age of six to nine months. A
male cat is capable of breeding at the
tender age of five months. The physical
development of these cats is, however,
much slower; a male Bombay is not fully
grown until the age of two.

How It All Began

The Bombay breed appeared in the
1950s. However, it does not originate
from Bombay, India, but rather the
United States. The first "mother" of the
breed, Nikki Horner, lived in Kentucky.
She was inspired by the black leopards
of India and decided to try and breed a
mini-panther of her own.

Inspired by Bagheera, the black
panther in Rudyard Kipling's *The
Jungle Book,* Horner dedicated her life
to creating a breed that resembled the
black jungle cat. She wanted a cat breed
with excellent muscles, suppleness, and
elegance that could be compared to
that of the panther's. She achieved her
goal, and in 1976, the Cat Fanciers'
Association accepted the breed for
championship status.

Kanaani

Build: large

Head: broad triangle

Eyes: wide set, slightly slanted, almond shaped, large, wide eyed, green

Body: large, lean, muscular

Tail: very long and thin, stronger at the base, tapering, black tip with at least three rings

Coat: short, tight; fine undercoat; firm structure

Color: base color from beige to cinnamon with seal, chocolate, or cinnamon colored spots (ticked fur) or marbled

This is a pedigree cat with a wildcat appearance.

"Those like me, who love cats, and love to observe them, who live in Canaan (today part of Israel), will discover these semiwild animals living in certain areas; at first glance—or perhaps at the layman's second glance—these cats resemble the original wildcat (*Felis lybica*)," said the now deceased founder of the Kanaani breed, Doris Pollatschek.

The cat lover enthusiastically described the ferocity and valor of these slender, long-legged animals with large, wide-set ears and elegant long necks and tails: "I found it very pleasing, this swift little hunter who discovered jerboa, lizards, giant beetles, and also the nests of ground-nesting birds hidden away. What a primitive animal to have in the house! What a wonderful and very selfish idea!" Pollatschek's dream became a reality when the Kanaani breed was officially recognized in 2000 by the World Cat Federation.

It All Began With Simmy

It was Simmy, one of the semiwild cats, that lay the foundation stone for this experimental breed. When Pollatschek had a visit from some of her Israeli friends, they recognized Simmy as a hybrid—half house cat, half wildcat. Apparently, this is quite a common concept in Israel. The muscular body, characteristic eyes, and extremely long, thin tail are simply unmistakable characteristics, as well as the wide-set ears that emphasize the triangular head shape, giving this cat a unique appeal.

Oriental Wedding

So what happened next with this breed? A backcrossing (crossing a hybrid with its parent or an animal genetically similar to its parent) of the protected wildcat was out of the question for the breeder, so she decided on a mating with an elegant Oriental shorthair. The first generation of hybrids already showed the desired long, strong bodies, but the heads and tails did not meet expectations.

"Above all, they were simply not cats who were happy to remain in the house. This generation of cats had an irrepressible urge to be outside," recalled Pollatschek, who watched the mother cat teach her seven-week-old kittens how to climb an eleven-and-a-half-foot fence.

A Tame Wildcat

After eight crossings, none of which were inbreeding, Pollatschek had a reason to be proud of herself and her cats: the crossing of spotted Orientals (ideal body shape and ear size), Abyssinians (golden nature, good head and ear shape), and Bengals (excellent muscularity, jumping and climbing

abilities, and size) created a cat breed that looked amazingly similar to the wildcat.

The WCF standard emphasizes that the Kanaani was bred to look like the confident spotted wildcat (*Felis lybica Gordoni*) as much as possible. The characteristic, predatory gait and a breathtaking talent for jumping are considered to be prominent features of the breed. They feel a strong need for independence, but although this looks like a wildcat, it is certainly not lacking in charm or affection.

Crossing With Domestic Breeds

So Doris Pollatschek had bred a real wildcat, but she quickly realized that this idea was not a very realistic one. The Kanaani had to be suitable for family life and not lead a separate existence in an outdoor enclosure.

Crossing this breed with tamer breeds proved to be a possibility, in order to create a cuddly cat with a wildcat appearance. After several years of exciting experimental breeding with many ups and downs, Pollatschek was sure of one thing: "Originally, I believed that one could easily tame hybrids or wildcats. This is probably only true after many generations, and unfortunately I did not have as much time as the ancient Egyptians."

Selkirk Rex

Build: large, stocky

Head: rounded, solid, broad skull with large chin; short, wide, straight nose

Eyes: large and round, deep set; color should correspond with coat color

Body: medium to large, muscular, stocky; large chest, shoulders, and back

Tail: medium length, thick, rounded tip

Coat: short, plushy, double coated; dense undercoat; pronounced waves

Colors: all colors and colorpoints are recognized

A gentle, shaggy-coated cat

These curious cats are littered with funny curls all over their bodies. The Selkirk rex, a recognized breed since 1987, is considered to be an ideal domestic house cat that integrates very well into a family. Fans of this breed describe these tousled teddy bears as loving, easygoing, intelligent, fascinating, and different. What more could you want? A cat with a distinctive playfulness, perhaps? Well this American breed can offer this, too. Play is very important to these cats, and they love to frolic around and perform daredevil stunts. This resourceful cat simply loves to be on the move. It is a good idea to provide him with lots of toys and a scratching post.

Pedigree

Because the Selkirk rex is still a relatively new breed, crossings are still permitted. Persians and British shorthairs have added to the gene pool of this breed, and the CFA standard has also permitted the crossbreeding of exotic shorthairs. Selkirk rex cats born before January 1, 1998, did not need to declare their relationship to the American shorthair. From 2010, however, only Selkirk or British shorthair parents are allowed. From 2015, Selkirks are only permitted to be mated with other Selkirks. Then it will be seen whether this breed can stand on its own four paws.

The breeding aims to produce a cat with a squat, stocky build, more reminiscent of a British shorthair than a Persian. The scattered curls adorn a rounded yet muscular body. Well, that is the theory anyway. The reality is still slightly different. Selkirks have many different types of fur; some have fine fur, others have thick fur, and both short and long fur also exists in this breed.

The chic curls do require some care; otherwise, they can become tangled. Specimens with a fine coat

should be groomed daily, and for cats with a coarser coat, once a week is sufficient.

Origins In an Animal Shelter

It all started in an animal shelter in Montana. A small house cat with an unusual coat attracted the attention of the manager. A local breeder adopted her and named the curly cat Miss DePesto. Out of sheer curiosity, the breeder mated her Persian cat with this now fully grown curly cat. Three of the six kittens from this litter had curly fur, and there was also one kitten with long fur as well. The breeder had never seen the combination of long fur and curls; this was the beginning of the breeding program.

Backcrossing these cats resulted in tragedy: most of the kittens from the litter died within a few weeks from allergic reactions, which also happened to subsequent litters during the pioneer breeding stage. But the breeders did

not give up. The number of Selkirks has grown fairly rapidly since 1995. Widening the gene pool is very much in the forefront of breeders' minds, and so long as there are responsible breeders, they will strive to breed out the problems of this breed, making them a thing of the past.

Thai

Build: medium

Head: rounded; emphasized cheeks and forehead

Eyes: medium size, wide set; almond-shaped upper eyelid, rounded bottom eyelid

Body: medium size, solid, well structured; well developed, strong muscles

Tail: in proportion to the body, wider at the base than at the tip

Coat: dense, coarse, lies flat against body

Color: seal point, blue point, chocolate point, lilac point, red point, tortoiseshell point, tabby point

This is a breed with more than a passing resemblance to the Siamese cat.

If you were to look into the deep blue eyes of a Thai cat, you would feel as though you were looking at a Siamese cat from the breeding scene in the 1950s. With its rounded yet angular head, this large, solid cat is reminiscent of the original Siamese cat, whose appearance has little in common with the modern Siamese cat. A modern Siamese is characterized by its wedge-shaped head, extreme slenderness, long legs, slim limbs, and narrow tail. Thai cats, also called old-style Siamese and traditional Siamese, are more robustly built. Balanced, generous proportions and strong muscles give them an athletic physique. Their rounded head shape is particularly striking and meant that Thai cats were referred to as "appleheads" in the United States.

Elegant and Slender

In the early 1960s, the first change to the Siamese breed took place. An increasing number of judges and breeders favored the extremely slender Siamese cats. Many breeders of the old type left cat shows feeling disappointed. Times had changed, and their cats had no chance of success. This trend continued for almost twenty years. It was only in 1986 that the old type of Siamese was shown in exhibitions in the United States. This turnaround is the result of the tireless work of a few breeders who wish to stay true to the original Siamese so that this breed is not lost forever. A small circle of breeders, predominantly in the United States, considered the more extreme form of the modern Siamese as dubious and decided to make it their responsibility to initiate a counter-breeding. Followers of the traditional Siamese cat breed aimed to recreate a specimen as seen in cat shows in the 1950s. The founders of the Traditional Cat Association (TCA) helped with the mission of preventing these cats from becoming extinct. Because there was only a very limited number of cats

deemed suitable to continue the breed, it was necessary to draw on the help of an outcross program. The crossing with European shorthairs led to a change in the slender Oriental type. The Tonkinese cat also helped return the Siamese to its original appearance. The American breeders did some excellent pioneering work; within a relatively short space of time, they bred cats that almost fully corresponded to the original type.

While the breeding work was in full swing, the recognition of the Thai cat was soon to follow. In 1990, the United States standard was also officially recognized in Germany by the World Cat Federation (WCF). The WCF also recognized all clubs affiliated with the Thai cat.

Purring Rascals

Thai cats are devoted to their people. These cats capture the hearts of their humans with their irresistible charm, loud purr, and lively temperament. This breed is intelligent, friendly, and talkative—all characteristics that have won him many fans. However, Thai cats can be little rascals. If you do not give your Thai cat enough attention, he will find another way to take center stage. Thai cats are sociable beings; they like to live in a group of cats, and they tolerate other pets very well. With patience, love, and plenty of treats, a Thai cat can accomplish almost anything. When the mood takes him, he can learn quite a few tricks!

Ceylon

Build: small

Head: rounded, short, broad; pronounced cheekbones; slightly flattened forehead; slightly curved profile

Eyes: large, wide set, yellow or green

Body: small to medium

Tail: short, powerful, rounded tip

Coat: very short, fine, silky texture, close fitting

Color: uniform background color; color varies from sand to gold depending on ticking; black, blue, red, cream, tortoiseshell, and blue-cream are recognized ticking colors

This is a cat for quiet people who want peace.

Ceylons are rare gems, silky with a short coat that just invites you to stroke it. The black-ticked beauties hail from the island of Sri Lanka and resemble Abyssinians, at least in terms of their fur. The Singapura, which is not recognized by all cat associations, is a close genetic relative of the Ceylon. All three of these breeds are characterized by their distinctive ticked fur. Ceylons are not recognized by FIFe.

The ticked fur of a Ceylon is a vital characteristic. Bentota is one variant, where the basic genetic color of the body matches the banding on the face, legs, and tail, but the main feature is the tabby stripes on the fur. This variant can also have a characteristic ruff. Ceylon black-ticked cats without stripes are known as the Manilla variant. In the Chaus variant, the ticking extends all the way down to the tail. Red, blue, cream, and tortoiseshell are further recognized colors. Currently, Ceylons with all-over tabby markings are not allowed to be bred, presumably because of the fear that the characteristics of the breed might be lost in doing so.

To retain the purity of this magnificent breed, there have been no outcross programs. Not all breeding with other breeds is excluded, however; an import of variants of the Ceylon breed from Sri Lanka, the Ceylon's country of origin, has been planned. Unfortunately, not all of these cats match the ideal breed. Some common shortcomings include tail deformities.

If this breeding goes ahead as planned, a selective approach will be required.

A Little Cat

Ceylons are relatively small cats, although there are some medium-sized specimens as well. The shoulders and hips are well developed, and the broad chest proves that, despite her modest size, this springy little tiger is not as fragile as she looks.

This exotic, cuddly pet has long, slender legs and would certainly appreciate a large cat tree with plenty of fancy climbing features. She likes to balance at dizzying heights, and this ability is enhanced by her short, powerful tail with a rounded tip.

The sensitive and sometimes headstrong Ceylon has very prominent cheekbones. A slightly curved profile gives the cat a focused yet sweet expression.

But what would the Ceylon be without her large, wide-set eyes that observe strangers with a great curiosity? The upper eyelid is almond shaped while the lower has rounded contours. Bright yellow or bright green eyes are the typical eye colors of this rare beauty.

A Coat Like Silk

A close-fitting coat with a silky texture is an important criterion of the Ceylon. It should be short and fine. A fine undercoat is another characteristic of the breed.

The Ceylon has a uniform color all over. The color of the ticking varies from sand to gold. A lack of tabby markings on the legs, tail, and tummy is seen as a serious mistake of the breed. This also applies to white, if it extends beyond the chin and neck.

103

Other WCF Breeds

Many of the breeds recognized by the World Cat Federation (WCF) are also accepted by the Fédération International Féline (FIFe). However, the WCF recognizes more breeds than the older federation. Apart from those presented in the previous chapters, there are many other breeds that you will find mentioned briefly in the collection below.

York

Yorks are medium-sized, long-bodied cats with well-developed muscles and a solid bone structure. Their coat is medium length, lustrous, and fine.

The stunning Tonkinese has delicate coloring.

According to the WCF breed standard, this cat is recognized exclusively in the colors chocolate and lilac, as well as both of these colors with a white front. The eyes are golden, hazel, or green.

Asian

All tabby colors for this medium-sized breed are allowed. Yellow and amber eyes complete the picture. The Asian's coat is very short, fine, and glossy. It fits close to the body and has almost no undercoat. The underside of the body is lighter than the rest. Contrasting dark colorpoints are desirable.

Australian Mist

The fur of the green-eyed Australian mist is short, shiny, and springy. The standard requires a rich, warm reddish brown tint on the nose, cheeks, and ears. The colors chocolate, lilac, caramel, gold (cinnamon), and peach (fawn) develop in the first two years of life. Spotted or marbled patterns are desirable.

Brazilian Shorthair

Large, high-set eyes and an extreme distance between the pupils are the hallmark of the Brazilian shorthair. The short, tight-fitting coat has no undercoat. A silky texture and a wonderful shine are typical of the breed. For Brazilian shorthairs, all colors except colorpoints are allowed.

Don Sphynx

As hairless cats, these unusual beauties have springy, elastic skin that may be covered in a fine down. Wrinkles on the head, neck, legs, and on the belly are desirable as well as whiskers. The paws should have long toes, which are

**The Savannah is a young
breed that is on its way to
being recognized.**

sometimes called "monkey fingers." For
this breed, all colors are permitted; there
is no conventional color for these cats.

Celtic Shorthair

Behind this name hides nothing other
than the cat breed that is known as the
European shorthair by the FIFe. Any
crossings from this breed are undesirable.
The Celtic shorthair corresponds to
an average European domestic, which
has developed without following any
conscious breeding rules.

Singapura

This is a small but compactly built breed.
The ears are notable for their large size
and the bright tufts of fur in the inner
ears. The eyes are large and expressive,
varying from yellowish green to yellow
to hazel. The short, dense fur has a sepia
agouti coloring. The base color is ivory
with a warm brown banding.

Peterbald

This is another naked cat with soft,
elastic skin. The head in particular has
lots of wrinkles, less so on the body.
Peterbald cats should not be bred with
sphynx cats. Crossing with Siamese,
Balinese, Oriental shorthair, and
Oriental longhair breeds is permitted,
however.

Tonkinese

These cats are a dream for fans of
delicate colors. Natural mink, champagne
mink, blue mink, platinum mink, and
honey mink are recognized colors
according to the WCF breed standard.
The fur of this cat appears as if it has
been given a coat of gloss. The underside
of the body is always slightly brighter
than the rest. Patterns and stripes are
undesirable; however, the points are
permitted to be a little darker than the
rest of the coat.

Living With a Pedigreed Cat

Finding a Reputable Breeder

So your decision has been made. You want a kitten, and not just any kitten, but a pedigreed one from a good home. You want your new cat to not only be purebred but to also be in good health and not have any viruses or other illness. But where do you find a cat breeder who takes welfare, responsible matings, hygiene, care, love, and devotion seriously? There are several large organizations and clubs run by breeders. Unfortunately, the sheer value of pedigreed cats has given run to a flood of organizations, and you must choose one that you feel is trustworthy. If you are not familiar with the cat breeding scene, it is best to choose a prestigious and established association, such as the Cat Fanciers' Association. Generally speaking, these will offer you competent advice and be able to put you in touch with the relevant breeder.

Often there are also communities within the different breeding associations that give specialized, valuable advice and information along the way.

Exhibitions

Cat shows are a great way to meet cat breeders. Almost every weekend in any number of different event halls, there are cat shows being organized. You can request an events calendar from relevant magazines or the relevant breeding association.

At an exhibition, you can only form a superficial impression of a cat breeder, but at the very least, you will find some breeders who give you the right impression and some who may not. If the breeder you feel is right also has a clean living environment for his or her cats, these are ideal conditions for your cat purchase.

˅ One sign of a good breeder is a tame mother cat.

If you find a breeder who leaves you with the right impression and breeds your desired breed, you could swap numbers and agree on an appointment. It is essential to visit the breeder's home to be sure that he or she keeps and breeds his or her animals humanely. Also, the health of the cats in the breeder's household must be impeccable.

Classifieds

The classified advertisements section in professional magazines is another resource for breeders' contact details. They are usually sorted by breed and can be found quickly and easily in the right section of the magazine. The first contact will generally be by phone or e-mail, then followed by a personal visit to the breeder. Do not be shy in asking for a picture of the litter (by e-mail, for example) because if you do not, you will not be sure if this kitten is the one you are looking for—her description may not be entirely accurate. It pays to choose your breeder very carefully right from the start in order to prevent disappointment.

The Purchase Agreement

A person who purchases a kitten from a reputable breeder will have to sign a purchase agreement. This is the beginning of most cat-human relationships, deeply unromantic though it may be. Despite your excitement about your new family member, your parents will need to carefully read the agreement, and if in doubt, consult with a lawyer before the document is signed.

"Not all laymen contracts are legally binding. If the breeder does not issue an official form, for example, from a responsible breeding association, it is advisable in any case, to consult a professional prior to signing," recommend lawyers.

A Written or Spoken Contract?

In general, purchase agreements are drawn up in writing. Although verbal agreements can be legally binding, they often do not have the desired outcome. If your parents do make a spoken agreement, they should have neutral witnesses present, and these people should not be associated with either party. They should have no relationship of dependency to the buyer or seller.

107

If the kitten changes hands, additional arrangements should be agreed upon in order to protect the animal. Many breeders write up a before and after purchase agreement to prohibit the kitten from being resold. This prevents the kitten from falling into the hands of a dealer or being resold privately to someone else. Bans on breeding, probation periods, and special designations such as "breeding or show animal" could also be noted in the contract.

Adoption Agreement

Adoption contracts are usually issued when you rescue an animal from an animal shelter or an animal protection society. The well-being of the animal is the central focus of this contract. Therefore, an adoption agreement is drawn that includes terms on welfare, behavior, competent care, medical care, and a donation. The rights of the animal shelter or animal welfare organization are outlined here. Otherwise, adoption contracts have an identical content to purchase contracts.

Basic Needs

Cats, just like people, have certain basic needs. So before you bring your four-legged friend home, here are some of the things you will need to buy:
> litter box
> litter and litter scoop
> cat food (wet and dry food)
> treats
> cat grass
> food and water bowls (stainless steel or lead-free ceramic, not plastic)
> carrier (ideally a plastic box with a detachable top section)
> claw clippers, brushes, combs (according to the fur texture of the cat)
> cat shampoo
> cat tree/scratching post (sturdy and stable)
> toys (no small parts or sharp edges)
> cat bed

To prevent any problems, it is highly recommended that your parents and the breeder draw up a written contract, since a spoken contract can lead to too many pitfalls.

What Should Be in the Contract?

A contract defines the rights and obligations of the two contracting parties. In order for this contract to be legally binding, the following must be included:
> Name and address of the seller
> Name and address of the buyer
> Specification of the animal of purchase (breed, color, sex, pedigree registration number, name)
> Summary of the purchase price
> Date and signature of the seller
> Date and signature of the buyer

Vaccinations and Deworming

Your cat will need to be vaccinated and dewormed on a regular basis. The following routine usually applies:

Core Vaccinations (suggested for all cats)

> Panleukopenia (feline distemper)/feline calicivirus and feline herpesvirus: first dose as early as six weeks old, then every three to four weeks until sixteen weeks of age; a booster given one year later, then every three years

> Rabies: one dose from eight to twelve weeks of age, revaccinate one year later; a booster given annually or every three years depending on local or state law

Non-Core Vaccinations (suggested for cats with high risk of exposure)

> Feline leukemia: first dose from eight to twelve weeks old and second dose three to four weeks later; a booster given one year later, then annually

> Feline immunodeficiency virus: first dose as early as eight weeks of age, then two doses at two- to three-week intervals; a booster given one year later, then annually

> Chlamydophila: first dose as early as nine weeks old, then a second dose three to four weeks later; annual booster

> Bordetella: first dose at eight weeks of age, then second dose two to four weeks later; annual booster

ᐯ Cat toys belong on the list of basic things you need to buy for your new cat.

Deworming

> At two to three weeks old, then at five to six weeks of age; the veterinarian may recommend deworming every month until six months old.

Grooming and Hygiene

Though cats are naturally very clean animals, they do not always manage to keep on top of their grooming without human help. Cats with very long fur do need assistance; the Persian is particularly maintenance-intensive and requires the regular use of special brushes and combs. Short-haired and semilonghair cats are also in need of care. Checking eyes, teeth, and claws all belong to your cat care regime no matter what the breed.

Pet stores offer a variety of grooming supplies. For longhairs and semilonghairs, it is best to use brushes with curved metal bristles. Fine-tooth combs complete the finer grooming work. Persians need daily grooming, while Norwegian forest cats usually only need a thorough brushing once a week. Use a natural bristle brush, which makes the fur shine.

Short-haired breeds with silky coats can be well groomed with a rubber-studded brush. If the cat has a dense undercoat, use a curved metal brush and a blunt-tooth comb. Breeds with no undercoat can be groomed using a fine-tooth comb.

If you would like to own a rex cat or a similar breed, bear in mind that these breeds have extremely sensitive skin. For grooming, you should only use a special rubber pad or soft brush to prevent skin irritation or even injury.

Show cats will need to take baths, which benefit their fur and general appearance, although they may not particularly like it! So as long as you do not overdo it, there is nothing wrong with giving your cat a bath, but if you are not exhibiting your cat, then spare him the ordeal. However, if he gets paint, oil, or a similar harmful substance on himself, then a bath is unavoidable. You will need a special cat shampoo for this. Once he has had his bath, make sure he stays in a draft-free, heated room to dry.

Eyes and Ears

Eyes and ears should be regularly checked for dirt, goop, and parasites. Your veterinarian can give you a special cleaning lotion to clean the corners of the eyes and also the ears. Usually the solution can be easily applied to a piece of cotton and gently rubbed over the affected area. Do not use cotton swabs to clean ears and eyes because this could injure your pet.

Powder and Shampoo

There are several reasons to use shampoo and powder. Long-haired cats with straight fur tend to get matted clumps in their coats. To correct this unsightly problem, you can buy a special powder that you put behind the ears, in the armpits, in the groin, and at the base of the tail.

▲ Ears and eyes should
be kept clean.

▼ Persian cats require
intensive grooming.

Dental Care

Take a look in your cat's mouth to see whether he
has any tartar or gum inflammation. If you notice
any changes, consult your veterinarian. The vet can
also teach you how to brush your cat's teeth with a
special tiny toothbrush or finger brush and cat-safe
toothpaste. Never use toothpaste made for humans!

Basic Care

Basic care refers to all the things you as the owner
will have to do to maintain your cat's health,
including grooming his coat. Persian owners
need to set aside some time every day to maintain
a routine. If these long-haired beauties are not
groomed daily, their fur will become tangled and
knotted quite quickly, resulting in skin lesions,
parasites, and other diseases. For cat shows, of

course, you will need to spend a lot more time grooming and washing him before taking him to the show. For regular Persian owners, such intensive measures are only required in exceptional cases. For basic care, you will need the following items:

> a wide-tooth comb
> a fine-tooth comb
> a wire brush (use only on the chest area)
> a soft toothbrush (for the face)
> cotton balls (for the eyes)
> powder (for greasy fur)
> nail clippers (for occasional claw clipping)

The wide-tooth comb is used to get rid of any loose fur and to prevent knotting. First untangle any knots with your fingers before you comb them through. The armpits and the genital area require special attention because tangles form quickly in these places and dirt can settle. If there are any specks of feces around the genital area, gently comb them out and then apply powder. Powder binds to the odor and prevents

the area from becoming contaminated. If there is any contamination, fresh powder can help dry out the area, then you can comb this out. First use a wide-tooth comb, then use the fine-tooth comb to finish. Make sure you groom your Persian's tail carefully because the fur is easily ripped from the tail and takes a very long time to grow back.

Cleaning the Face

A Persian's face should be maintained on a daily basis because eye secretions and uneaten food may get stuck in the fur and lead to unsightly discoloration of the fur.

To care for the eyes, use a damp, but not wet, cotton ball and gently rub the bridge of the nose and under the eyes to remove any encrustations. Instead of just using water, you can buy a special cleaning solution from your veterinarian.

You can also use this method to remove any food that has become stuck anywhere on the face. Wet the fur on the face and apply powder or rice starch with your fingers. Allow time for the powder to soak up the dampness from the fur and then brush it out using a soft toothbrush.

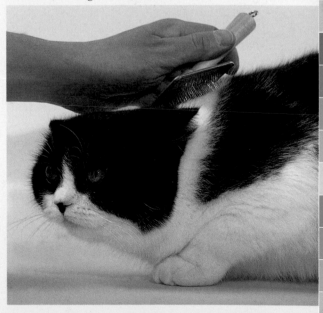

Claw Care

Cats have sharp claws that need to be worn down regularly or they become too long. Young cats that go outside regularly or cats with sufficient scratching posts do not usually need help with claw care. For old or ill cats or cats that do not get regular exercise, this is somewhat different. The description below will show you how to trim your cat's claws if and when necessary.

Trimming your cat's claws is a touchy subject. Most vets recommend—and rightly so—that this should be left to the professionals. Each claw has a fine nerve, called the quick, that can be damaged if the claw is not cut carefully. For the cat, this means incredible pain and a fear of having his claws cut in the future. So if you are feeling extra cautious, you should entrust claw care to your vet.

Doing It Yourself

Whether you decide to cut your cat's claws yourself or take him to a vet, the same applies: slowly and carefully get your cat used to this procedure, and use a calm approach so that he does not become defensive. Be patient and above all, avoid trimming the claw too far down or you will cut the quick.

Paws

Place your cat on a towel spread out on a table or have him sitting on your lap. Now pat him lovingly, scratch his neck, and gently work your way down to his paws. If your cat becomes restless, talk to him in a reassuring manner. Now try to raise the forepaw with one hand, and use the other hand to offer him a treat. Hold the paw only briefly at first, then extend this time and reward him with more treats.

Inspecting the Claws

Once the cat is used to having his paw held for some time, gently spread the toes apart, and with your thumb resting on the top of the paw, put your index and middle fingers on the footpads. Use very slight pressure to unsheathe the claws and examine them. Remember to start very slowly and increase the period of observation gradually so you do not upset your fluffy friend. Offer him a treat immediately after you have finished examining his claws.

Claw Clippers

Cutting the claws is best done with a special clipper you can buy from your veterinary practice or a pet supply store. There are two kinds of claw trimmer: the guillotine and scissors. Some find the guillotine-style clipper easier to use.

▼ a guillotine-style claw clipper

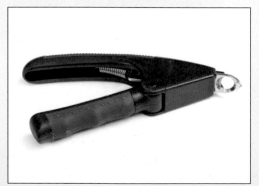

▼ a scissors-style claw clipper

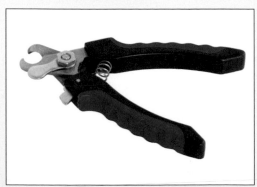

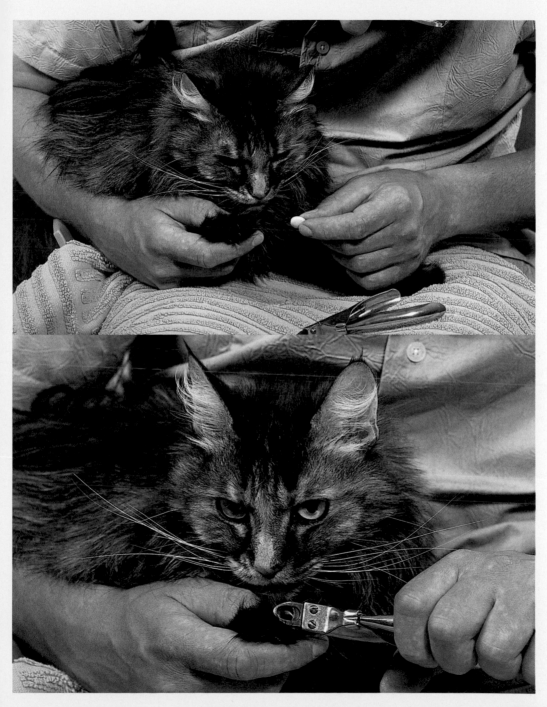

But no matter which style of clipper you choose, your cat must get used to this special tool. Place it within your cat's view and let her sniff it; stroke her while she does this. Gradually move the claw clippers closer to your cat, as long as she is not upset by them. Reward her with treats so that she associates the clippers with something positive.

Clipping

For the last stage of her habituation training, place the clippers on her claws without actually cutting them so your cat gets used to them touching her claws. Place the clippers on each claw individually then reward her with a treat. After this, you will find it much easier to clip her claws, and she will have no reason to fear the clippers. If you want to cut your cat's claws yourself then be very careful not to injure her. Make sure you use a good source of light so you can see where the nerves are and avoid cutting them.

Traveling With Your Cat

You may need to occasionally transport your cat in the car with you. She will have had her first experience of this when you brought her home from the breeder or shelter. Perhaps you need to take her to the vet for her annual checkups or to the cattery (cat-boarding facility) when you go on vacation.

Most house cats, by nature, do not have a fear of traveling in the car, provided they have never had a bad experience with this means of transport. If this is not the case, then the cat may emit a miserable or angry yowl. Some cats may even soil themselves in the car or start drooling if they are very afraid. However, a reaction such as this is the exception. In most cases, after a few protests, the cat will calm down and sit quietly, and the carrier will remain relatively clean after the car ride.

Safety

Safety is paramount when it comes to road trips with your cat. Do not allow her to just roam freely around in the car. What may seem okay at first glance could actually be fatal. Unsecured cats can not only distract the driver of the car and thus increase the risk of accidents, but sometimes cats panic and jump on the driver, on the wheel, or under the pedals.

Plastic Cat Carrier

A sturdy plastic carrier with a lockable door is still considered to be the safest option when it comes to transporting your four-legged friend from one place to another. These boxes are not only easy to carry, but they are also easy to clean. You should get your cat used to her pet carrier before the journey so she feels completely comfortable. Simply place the carrier with the door open in a place your cat is familiar with and put a fluffy towel inside. If you make the interior of the crate really comfortable, it will not be long before your cat climbs in for a cozy nap.

No Drafts

During the journey, make sure there are no drafts in the car. Cats can get cold very easily if there is a harsh breeze blowing into the car. During hot summer months, cats should never be left alone in the car because the interior can heat up quickly and become a death trap.

Cat Associations

Granted, the variety of cat associations and clubs is confusing. On closer inspection, however, it is a fairly small structure—at least, as long as you stick to the main organizations. For the purposes of clarity, the following list is not exhaustive:

The World Cat Congress (WCC)

The World Cat Congress is an umbrella organization made up of representatives of various confederations. The success story of the WCC began in 1994, quite by accident. The Italian cat association, Associazione Nationale Felina Italiana (ANFI), organized an event called "Cats and Man." There were many artistic, literary, and scientific contributions that made this event very special. The event also had an international exhibition and this brought leading figures of various umbrella organizations together: Don Williams, president of the Cat Fanciers' Association (CFA) from the United States; Brenda Wolstenholme from the Governing Council of the Cat Fancy (GCCF) of the United Kingdom; Alvia Uddin, president of the Fédération International Féline (FIFe); and Anneliese Hackmann, president of the World Cat Federation (WCF). This was an ideal opportunity to get together and gain a better understanding and cooperation between the various confederations.

They decided to meet regularly from that point on to talk more about their organizations. There were also veterinary seminars, panel discussions on current issues, breed presentations, and an exhibition directed by the leaders of the international federations.

The stated theme of the World Cat Congress is to promote anything to do with the welfare of cats, an issue that is not only at the heart of breeders but every cat lover as well. The World Cat Congress meets once a year in various different countries.

The Fédération Internationale Féline (FIFe)

As a worldwide governing body, FIFe represents forty-two organizations from forty different countries. Its membership numbers approximately seventy-five thousand cat lovers. All members adhere to FIFe standards: the individual breed standards, official recognition of the breeds, exact exhibition sequences, as well as the judges and the one hundred fifty candidate judges.

It all began with a Frenchwoman named Marguérite Ravel. The cat lover dreamed of a European umbrella organization to establish cat clubs that would enjoy international recognition. A meeting of the Royal Cat Society of Flanders (Belgium), the French Cat Federation, and the Italian Cat Society on the Seine River in France in 1949 saw the unofficial founding of the Fédération Internationale Féline d'Europe (FIFE).

That same year, FIFE organized the first cat show in Paris, where two hundred animals were exhibited. Exhibitors came from France, Italy, Switzerland, Belgium, and the Netherlands. By today's standards, this would be a minor show, considering in the past few years, the presence of more than fourteen hundred cats from all over the world is quite standard. In 1950, the first general assembly of the federation was held and the statutes and rules for exhibiting adopted. To commemorate the special event, each delegate present at the first general assembly was given a pink sandstone sculpture of a cat, the work of a famous French sculptor, Jean Martel.

The association continued to grow and with the joining of Clubo Brasileiro de Gato (Brazilian Cat Club) in 1972, the Fédération Internationale Féline d'Europe outgrew European borders. It became the Fédération Internationale Féline (FIFe) during the following year's general assembly and took up the cause of the health and welfare of pedigreed cats.

Currently there are about two hundred international judges active at FIFe, supplemented with twenty national judges. There are also one hundred fifty candidate judges, and approximately eighty thousand pedigrees are issued and two thousand new kennel names registered per year. Around one hundred twenty-five thousand cats are shown at three hundred fifty exhibitions every year.

The World Cat Federation (WCF)

Five hundred forty individual organizations from around the world, including the United States, belong to the World Cat Federation (WCF), the Germany-based umbrella organization. The tasks of the WCF include:

> international kennel protection registrations
> education, training, and examination of international judges
> standard definitions of all breeds
> creation of show rules and classes
> formation of international contacts

The Cat Fanciers' Association (CFA)

The Cat Fanciers' Association (CFA) is the largest registry of pedigreed cats in the world. It was founded back in 1906. That same year, the first exhibitions attracted cat lovers to Buffalo, New York, and Detroit, Michigan. In 1907, the first Annual General Meeting took place at the famous Madison Square Garden in New York. Meanwhile, the CFA directed about four hundred exhibitions all over the world. The principal office of the CFA is in Alliance, Ohio.

Other Associations

> Governing Council of the Cat Fancy (GCCF)
> American Association of Cat Enthusiasts (AACE)
> Australian Cat Federation (ACF)
> American Cat Fanciers Association (ACFA)
> Canadian Cat Association/Association Féline Canadienne (CCA/AFC)
> Cat Federation of Southern Africa (CFSA)
> Feline Control Council of Victoria, Australia (FCCV)
> New South Wales Cat Fanciers' Association (NSWCFA)
> Cat Fanciers' Federation (CFF)
> United Feline Association (UFO)
> The Traditional and Classic Cat International (TCCI)
> Traditional Cat Association (TCA)
> The International Cat Association (TICA)

< **Cat associations are dedicated to the genetic improvement and welfare of pedigreed cats.**

Questionnaire

Would a cat be happy to live with you? Are you a cat person? Not quite sure? Then please complete the following questionnaire before you decide to purchase a feline friend:

You are allowed to keep pets
in your home. ☐ Yes ☐ No

The whole family is in agreement
about owning a cat. ☐ Yes ☐ No

Your family members are allergy free. ☐ Yes ☐ No

You feel able to take responsibility for a
living creature for fifteen to twenty years. ☐ Yes ☐ No

You know someone who would care
for your cat if you go on vacation. ☐ Yes ☐ No

You know someone who would take care
of your cat if something happened to you. ☐ Yes ☐ No

You are willing to learn about your cat's
needs and apply your new knowledge. ☐ Yes ☐ No

Your family is willing to pay for
veterinary care for your cat and
possibly spend large sums. ☐ Yes ☐ No

You are prepared to undertake grooming
of your cat on a regular basis. ☐ Yes ☐ No

You accept the fact that your cat will
never be completely obedient. ☐ Yes ☐ No

Your family accepts the fact that the
house may become messy with cat toys
and fur on occasion. ☐ Yes ☐ No

Your family is prepared for scratches on furniture and curtains while the cat is being trained to use the scratching post.	▢ Yes	▢ No
You can accept the cat sleeping on your bed.	▢ Yes	▢ No
You are willing to clean up loose fur, vomit, urine, and feces.	▢ Yes	▢ No

Evaluation

› Did you answer more than three questions with a definite no? Then you should thoroughly reconsider the purchase of a cat. Ultimately you will most likely decide it is not for you.

› Did you answer all questions with an honest yes? Then there is nothing to stop you from realizing your dream of owning a cat! Have fun with your new companion!

Glossary

agouti—Banding of each individual hair due to the presence of a special gene.

bicolor—Solid or tabby with white markings; colored and white parts are evenly distributed, and a white blaze is desirable.

blotched tabby—A butterfly marking on the shoulders, with a pattern on the back that consists of a vertical line in the pattern color extending from the shoulder to the tail tip, and another line of color parallel on each side with clear contrast to the base color; on both sides of the body, there is a clearly visible swirling pattern. This pattern is also known as the marbled or classic tabby.

blue—A bluish gray color.

cat fancy—The community of cat breeders and cat lovers.

cattery—A kennel for cats.

chocolate—A dark brown.

chromosomes—Rod-shaped structures containing an organism's genes; they are found in the nuclei of cells.

cinnamon—A light brown color.

fawn—A light beige.

gene pool—All variations of the genes of a particular population.

guard hairs—The fur on the upper part of the coat.

harlequin—The coat pattern of bicolor or tricolor cats that is mostly white with colored spots on the body (three to five) and head.

hip dysplasia—A deformation of the hip joints.

hybrid—The product of the mating between different species or different cat breeds.

inbreeding—The mating of closely related animals, such as siblings or a parent with an offspring, with the aim of obtaining certain features.

lilac—A very light gray with a light pink shimmer.

markings—Patterned areas of fur that are darker than the base color.

mask—Darker-colored fur around the face.

mink—In pointed breeds, the body color is only a few shades lighter than the points.

mutation—Accidental genetic variation.

non-agouti—Solid-colored fur.

outcross—Describes the breeding of cats from different bloodlines.

phenotype—Physical appearance.

pheromone—A biological chemical that influences an animal's behavior.

points—Uniformly colored markings on the ears, paws, and tail (also on testicles in male cats) and a diamond-shaped mask completely covering the face, including whisker pads and chin, with traces of color on the ears; the back and belly (body color) are white to ivory in all different color variations.

recessive—Describes a gene in the animal that does not express itself as a feature; in contrast, a dominant gene does express itself physically.

red—Also called orange or ginger.

ruff—Longer fur around the neck than on the rest of the body. Also called a collar or mane.

seal—A very dark brown color.

shaded tabby—A coat pattern where the color extends about halfway down the hair shaft, and the rest of the hair shaft is white/ivory or golden. In a silver shaded tabby, the undercoat, chin, ear tufts, stomach, chest, insides of the legs, and the topside of tail are silvery white; the back, flanks, face, ears, tail, and outside upper legs have silver fur, evenly colored.

shell tabby—Also called chinchilla, only the tip of the hair shaft is colored while the rest of the hair is pale. In a silver shell tabby, the undercoat, chin, ear tufts, stomach, chest, insides of the legs, and underside of the tail are silvery white; the back, flanks, face, ears, topside of the tail, and outside upper legs have silver fur, evenly and lightly tipped. The fur has a sparkling appearance.

shirtfront—Longer fur on the chest than on the rest of the body.

smoke—Most of the hair shaft is colored with only a small band of pale fur near the root of the hair, which is only visible when the coat is parted or the cat is moving. Ear tufts, stomach, and tail underside are silver-white and the hair tips evenly colored.

solid—Fur is uniform in color from the hairline to the tip of tail and has no ghost markings (faint tabby markings on non-tabby cats).

sorrel—A red color similar to the coat of a fox.

stop—The indentation where the forehead meets the muzzle.

tabby—A coat with stripes, dots, lines, or swirls. All tabby markings are clear and equal on both sides of the body with markings (thumbprints) on the ears. In brindle, mackerel, spotted, and marbled tabbies there is an "M" on the forehead and two to three spirals on the cheeks. The chest should have two bands that should be unbroken, continuous markings. The legs have even stripes and the tail is evenly ringed. There is a double row of black spots from the chest to the stomach.

ticking—Every hair is banded three to five times with a colored tip. In some breeds, front and hind legs can have fine, clear stripes with one or two continuous or broken bands around the throat. For some breeds, stripes on the legs and chest are not permitted. The face and forehead have tabby markings; the rest of the body is free from markings. Stripes on the hind legs and on the tip of the tail are the same color as the markings.

tipping—Dark fur tips on a silver- or gold-colored base. Shell, shaded, and smoke are different degrees of tipping, from least to greatest, respectively.

tortie—Tortoiseshell.

tortoiseshell—A brindled coat with black and red patches, or lighter or darker variations (black/bright red, cinnamon/cream, blue/cream) over the entire body, including the extremities, and very little to no white; the calico pattern is mostly white with black and red patches.

tricolor—Tortoiseshell with white spotting; colored and white areas are evenly distributed, and a white blaze is desirable. Also called a calico.

trousers—Longer fur on the hind legs than on the rest of the body. Also called breeches or knickerbockers.

wild coloring—The base color is a dark apricot to dark orange with black ticking.

Further Reading

Books

The Complete Cat Breed Book. New York: DK Publishing, 2013.

Edwards, Alan. *The Ultimate Encyclopedia of Cats, Cat Breeds and Cat Care.* Lanham, Md.: Anness Publishing, 2012.

Helgren, J. Anne. *Encyclopedia of Cat Breeds.* Hauppauge, N.Y.: Barron's Educational Series, 2013.

Internet Addresses

The Cat Fanciers' Association
http://www.cfainc.org/home.aspx

Fédération Internationale Féline
http://fifeweb.org/index.php

World Cat Federation
http://www.wcf-online.de/

Index

A

Abyssinian, 36, 37, 38–39, 41, 63, 70, 71, 97, 102
adoption agreement, 108
American bobtail, 74
American Cat Fanciers Association (ACFA), 6, 49, 63, 66, 90, 119
American curl, 16, 18–19
American shorthair, 14, 41, 66, 67, 94, 98
Anatoli, 86, 92–93
Angora cat, 12, 24, 26, 29, 43, 59
animal shelter, 5, 99, 108
Asian, 104
Asian leopard cat, 40, 41
associations, 4, 6, 7, 9, 18, 25, 36, 49, 55, 76, 92, 102, 106, 107, 117–119

B

Balinese, 26, 76, 78–79, 80, 105
basic care, 112–113
basic needs, 108
Bengal, 37, 40–41, 62, 63, 97
Birman, 4, 10, 16, 24, 25, 26–27
Bombay, 86, 94–95
Brazilian shorthair, 104
breeders, 106–108
breeding regulations, 7
British blue, 37, 42, 43, 48–49, 60
British longhair, 86, 90–91

British shorthair, 37, 38, 42–43, 49, 77, 86, 87, 89, 90, 98
Burmese, 30, 36, 37, 44–45, 46, 47, 53, 77, 94
Burmilla, 37, 46–47

C

Carthusian (*see* British blue *and* Chartreux)
Cat Fanciers' Association (CFA), 6, 7, 9, 14, 18, 23, 26, 29, 49, 66, 71, 78, 95, 98, 106, 117, 119
Celtic shorthair, 105
Ceylon, 5, 38, 102–103
Chartreux, 37, 48, 49, 60
claw care, 114–116
Cornish rex, 36, 50–51, 52, 53, 87
Cymric, 74

D

dental care, 112
Devon rex, 36, 52–53, 58, 59, 73, 87
deworming, 109, 110
Don sphynx, 104–105

E

ear care, 111
Egyptian Mau, 41, 54–55, 62, 63
European shorthair, 37, 56–57, 101, 105
exotic shorthair, 5, 10–11, 14–15, 87, 98
eye care, 111

F

facial care, 113
Fédération Internationale Féline (FIFe), 4, 6, 7, 9, 10, 16, 18, 23, 29, 30, 35, 36, 37, 46, 48, 49, 50, 55, 61, 63, 71, 74, 76, 78, 86, 87, 102, 104, 105, 117–119

G

gender, 7, 8, 9
German rex, 36, 52, 53, 58–59, 87
grooming, 6, 10, 13, 14, 17, 19, 33, 80, 86, 91, 98–99, 110–116

H

Highland fold, 86, 88, 89

I

indoor cats, 5, 6, 15, 50, 52, 58
The International Cat Association (TICA), 6, 18, 49, 63, 66, 67, 90, 119

J

Japanese bobtail, 5, 36, 74–75
Javanese (*see* Oriental longhair)

K

Kanaani, 87, 96–97
Karelian bobtail, 74
Korat, 5, 60–61
Kurilian bobtail, 36, 74, 75

L

long-haired breeds, 4, 6, 111

M

Maine coon, 4, 9, 16, 17, 19, 20–21, 22, 28, 34
Manx, 5, 36, 61, 74, 75
Mekong bobtail, 74, 87
mixed-breed cats, 5, 6

N

neutering, 8, 9
Neva masquerade, 16, 30–31
Norwegian forest cat, 4, 16, 17, 19, 20, 22–23, 28, 34, 82, 110

O

ocicat, 37, 62–63
Oriental breeds, 15, 17, 21, 41, 44, 45, 76–85
Oriental longhair, 76, 80–81
Oriental shorthair, 4, 41, 76, 77, 80, 82–83, 87, 97, 105
outdoor cats, 6, 11, 17, 21, 22, 56

P

pedigree, 5, 6, 7, 10, 11, 12, 17, 28, 33, 47, 49, 56, 65, 70, 92, 93, 96, 98, 106, 118, 119
Persian, 4, 6, 10–11, 12–13, 14, 15, 16, 26, 28, 29, 33, 38, 43, 45, 47, 48, 53, 59, 76, 86, 87, 89, 90, 91, 98, 99, 110, 112, 113
Peterbald, 87, 105

R

ragdoll, 5, 16, 24–25, 31
Russian blue, 5, 10, 36, 37, 59, 60, 64–65, 77

S

safety, 117
scent marking, 8–9
Scottish fold, 5, 86, 88–89
Selkirk rex, 87, 98–99
semilonghair breeds, 6, 16–35, 36, 65, 70, 78, 80, 86, 87, 89, 110

short-haired breeds, 4, 6, 10, 13, 14, 15, 16, 18, 36–75, 86–87, 110
Siamese, 4, 18, 26, 30, 38, 43, 44, 45, 50, 53, 61, 63, 65, 66, 67, 70, 76, 78, 79, 82, 83, 84–85, 87, 89, 95, 100, 101, 105
Siberian forest cat, 16, 17, 20, 28–29, 30, 31
Singapura, 38, 102, 105
snowshoe cat, 37, 66–67
Sokoke, 37, 68–69
Somali, 5, 36, 38, 70–71
spaying, 8, 9, 83
sphynx, 36, 53, 72–73

T

tailless breeds, 74–75
Thai cat, 4, 30, 87, 100–101
titles (show), 7
traveling, 116–117
Tonkinese, 30, 87, 101, 105
Turkish Angora, 4, 12, 16, 17, 32–33, 35, 92, 93
Turkish Van, 16, 17, 34–35, 92, 93

V

vaccinations, 109

W

World Cat Federation (WCF), 6, 9, 51, 66, 74, 86, 87, 90, 92, 93, 96, 97, 101, 104, 105, 117, 119

Y

York, 104

English edition copyright © 2014 by Enslow Publishers, Inc.

All rights reserved.

No part of this book may be reproduced by any means without the written permission of the publisher.

Translated from the German edition by Claire Mullen.

Edited and produced by Enslow Publishers, Inc.

Originally published in German.

© 2006 Franckh-Kosmos Verlags-GmbH & Co. KG, Stuttgart, Germany

Gabriele Metz, *Katzenrassen: Alle Rassen und alle Farben*

Library of Congress Cataloging-in-Publication Data

Metz, Gabriele.

   [Katzenrassen. English]

   Get to know cat breeds : over 40 best-known breeds / Gabriele Metz.— English edition.

      pages cm. — (Get to know cat, dog, and horse breeds)

   Audience: 11-up.

   Audience: Grade 7 to 8.

      Summary: "Discusses the appearance, origin, and temperament of more than forty cat breeds grouped into categories established by the Fédération Internationale Féline (FIFe): Persians and exotic shorthairs, semi-longhair cats, short-haired cats and Somali, the Oriental family, and breeds recognized by the World Cat Federation (WCF). Includes a chapter on cat care"—Provided by publisher.

   Includes bibliographical references and index.

   ISBN 978-0-7660-4260-5

   1. Cat breeds—Juvenile literature. I. Title.

   SF445.7.M4813 2014

   636.8.—dc23

                       2013001608

Paperback ISBN 978-1-4644-0463-4

Printed in the United States of America

112013 Bang Printing, Brainerd, Minn.

10 9 8 7 6 5 4 3 2 1

To Our Readers: We have done our best to make sure all Internet addresses in this book were active and appropriate when we went to press. However, the author and publisher have no control over and assume no liability for the material available on those Internet sites or on other Web sites they may link to. Any comments or suggestions can be sent by e-mail to comments@enslow.com or to the address on the back cover.

Every effort has been made to locate all copyright holders of material used in this book. If any errors or omissions have occurred, corrections will be made in future editions of this book.

All information in this book is given to the best of the author's knowledge. However, care during implementation is still required. The publishers, authors, and translators assume no liability for personal injury, property damage, or financial loss as a result of the application of the methods and ideas presented in this book.

♻ Enslow Publishers, Inc., is committed to printing our books on recycled paper. The paper in every book contains 10% to 30% post-consumer waste (PCW). The cover board on the outside of each book contains 100% PCW. Our goal is to do our part to help young people and the environment too!

Photo Credits: Photographs by Gabriele Metz except Bent Aggersbol, Denmark, pp. 46, 47; Anita Engebakken, Denmark, pp. 68, 69; Pascal Pobé, France, p. 48 (bottom), Shutterstock.com, pp. 114, 125.

Cover Photo: Shutterstock.com (*main photo:* Persian; *from top to bottom:* Maine coon, American shorthair, Siamese, ragdoll).